WHAT'S COOKING

pasta

Tom Bridge

THUNDER BAY
P·R·E·S·S

This edition published in 1998 by
Thunder Bay Press
5880 Oberlin Drive, Suite 400
San Diego, California 92121-9653
1–800–284–3580

http:/www.adms web.com

Library of Congress Cataloging in Publication Data

Bridge, Tom.
  What's cooking? Pasta / Tom Bridge.
      p.   cm.
  Includes index.
  ISBN 1-57145-147-1
  1. Cookery (Pasta) I. Title.
TX 809. MI7B744   1988   98-3259
641.8'22--dc21   CIP

Printed in Italy

Produced by Haldane Mason, London

Acknowledgments
Art Director: Ron Samuels
Editorial Director: Sydney Francis
Editorial Consultant: Christopher Fagg
Managing Editor: Jo-Anne Cox
Editor: Linda A. Doeser
Design: Digital Artworks Partnership Ltd
Photography: Andrew Sydenham
Home Economist: Victoria Simister

Note
Unless otherwise stated, milk is assumed to be full fat, eggs are medium,
and pepper is freshly ground black pepper.

Contents

Introduction

Pasta has existed in one form or another since the days of the Roman Empire and remains one of the most versatile ingredients in the kitchen. It can be combined with almost anything from meat to fish, vegetables to fruit, and is even delicious served with simple herb sauces. No cupboard should be without a supply of dried pasta, which, combined with a few other stock ingredients, can be turned into a mouthwatering and nutritious meal within minutes.

Most pasta is made from durum wheat flour and contains protein and carbohydrates. It is a good source of slow-release energy and has the additional advantage of being value for money.

There is an enormous range of different types of pasta, some of which are listed on the opposite page. Many are available both dried and fresh. Unless you have access to a good, Italian delicatessen, it is probably not worth buying fresh unfilled pasta, but even supermarkets sell high-quality tortellini, capelletti, ravioli, and agnolotti.

Best of all, is to make fresh pasta at home. It takes a little time, but is quite easy and well worth the effort. You can mix the dough by hand or prepare it in a food processor.

Pasta may be colored and flavored with extra ingredients that are usually added with the beaten egg:

Black: add 1 tsp squid or cuttlefish ink.
Green: add 4 ounces well-drained, cooked spinach when kneading.
Purple: thoroughly process 1 large, cooked beet in a food processor, and add with an extra ½ cup flour.
Red: add 2 tbsp tomato paste.

Always use a large saucepan for cooking pasta and bring lightly salted water to a boil. Add the pasta and 1 tbsp olive oil, but do not cover or the water will boil over. Quickly bring the water back to a rolling boil and avoid overcooking. When the pasta is tender, but still firm to the bite, drain and toss with butter, olive oil, or your prepared sauce and serve as soon as possible.

The cooking times given here are guidelines only:

Fresh unfilled pasta:	*2–3 minutes*
Fresh filled pasta:	*8–10 minutes*
Dried unfilled pasta:	*10–12 minutes*
Dried filled pasta:	*15–20 minutes*

BASIC PASTA DOUGH

If you wish to make your own pasta for the dishes in this book, follow this simple recipe.

Serves 4

INGREDIENTS
4 cups durum wheat flour
4 eggs, lightly beaten
1 tbsp olive oil
salt

1 Lightly flour a counter. Sift the flour with a pinch of salt into a mound. Make a well in the center and add the eggs and olive oil.

2 Using a fork or your fingertips, gradually work the mixture until the ingredients are combined. Knead vigorously for 10–15 minutes.

3 Set the dough aside to rest for 25 minutes, before rolling it out as thinly and evenly as possible.

TYPES OF PASTA

There are as many as 200 different pasta shapes and about three times as many names for them. New shapes are being designed—and named—all the time, and the same shape may be called a different name in different regions of Italy.

anelli, anellini: *small rings for soup*

bucatini: *long, medium-thick tubes*

cannelloni: *large, thick, round pasta tubes*

capelli d'angelo: *thin strands of "angel hair"*

conchiglie: *ridged shells*

conchigliette: *little shells*

cresti di gallo: *curved-shaped*

ditali, ditalini: *short tubes*

eliche: *loose spirals*

farfalle: *bows*

fettuccine: *medium ribbons*

fusilli: *spirals*

gemelli: *two pieces wrapped together as "twins"*

lasagne: *flat, rectangular sheets*

linguini: *long, flat ribbons*

lumache: *snail-shaped shells*

lumaconi: *big shells*

macaroni: *long- or short-cut tubes*

orecchiette: *ear-shaped*

penne: *quill-shaped*

rigatoni: *thick, ridged tubes*

spaghetti: *fine or medium rods*

tagliarini: *thin ribbons*

tagliatelle: *broad ribbons*

vermicelli: *fine pasta, usually folded into skeins*

Cannelloni

Conchigliette

Fusilli

Conchiglie

Orecchiette tricolori

Rigatoni

Lumaconi

Fettuccine

Spaghetti

Soups & Light Meals

Pasta is so versatile: it can be used to make soups more substantial, as a delicious and unusual starter, or as a quick and easy lunch or light supper. The recipes in this chapter range from traditional Italian dishes, such as Minestrone soup and Spaghetti alla Carbonara, to intriguing new ways with pasta, such as Pancetta & Pecorino Cakes with Farfalle and Pasta Omelet.

Soup recipes include filling winter dishes that, if served with some crusty bread, make a meal in themselves. Try Navy Bean & Pasta Soup, for example. Others, like Cream of Lemon & Chicken Soup, are subtle and delicate. Recipes for snacks and light meals offer something for every taste—vegetable, cheese, meat, and fish sauces combined with every pasta shape from linguine to lumache. Try Smoked Ham Linguine if you are in a hurry, or Creamed Veal Kidneys with Penne if you want something a little different.

Minestrone

Italian cooks have created some very heartwarming
soups and this is the most famous of all.

Serves 8–10

INGREDIENTS

3 garlic cloves

3 large onions

2 celery sticks

2 large carrots

2 large potatoes

3¹/₂ ounces green beans

3¹/₂ ounces zucchini

4 tbsp butter

¹/₄ cup olive oil

2 ounces fatty bacon, finely diced

6⁷/₈ cups vegetable or
    chicken stock

1 bunch fresh basil, finely chopped

3¹/₂ ounces chopped tomatoes

2 tbsp tomato paste

3¹/₂ ounces Parmesan cheese rind

3 ounces dried spaghetti, broken up

salt and pepper

freshly grated Parmesan cheese,
    to serve

1 Finely chop the garlic, onions, celery, carrots, potatoes, beans, and zucchini using a sharp knife.

2 Heat the butter and oil together in a large saucepan, add the bacon and cook for 2 minutes. Add the garlic and onion and fry for 2 minutes, then add the celery, carrots, and potatoes and cook for a further 2 minutes, stirring the vegetables occasionally.

3 Add the beans to the saucepan and cook for about 2 minutes. Stir in the zucchini and cook for a further 2 minutes. Cover the pan and cook all of the vegetables, stirring frequently, for about 15 minutes.

4 Add the stock, basil, tomatoes, tomato paste, and cheese rind and season to taste. Bring to a boil, lower the heat and simmer for 1 hour. Remove and discard the cheese rind.

5 Add the spaghetti to the pan and cook for 20 minutes. Serve sprinkled with Parmesan.

COOK'S TIP

There are almost as many recipes for minestrone as there are cooks in Italy!
You can add almost any vegetables you like, including soaked dried beans.

Italian Cream of Tomato Soup

*Plum tomatoes are ideal for making soups and sauces, as
they have denser, less watery flesh than round varieties.*

Serves 4

INGREDIENTS

4 tbsp unsalted butter
1 large onion, chopped
2¹/₂ cups vegetable stock
2 pounds Italian plum tomatoes,
   skinned and roughly chopped
pinch of baking soda

2 cups dried fusilli
1 tbsp superfine sugar
⁵/₈ cup heavy cream
salt and pepper
fresh basil leaves, to garnish
deep-fried croûtons, to serve

1 Melt the butter in a large
saucepan, add the onion and
sauté for 3 minutes. Add 1¼ cups
of the vegetable stock to the
saucepan, with the chopped
tomatoes and baking soda. Bring
the soup to a boil and simmer for
20 minutes.

2 Remove the pan from the
heat and set aside to cool
slightly. Purée the soup in a
blender or food processor and
pour through a fine strainer back
into the saucepan.

3 Add the remaining vegetable
stock and the fusilli to the
pan, and season to taste with salt
and pepper.

4 Add the sugar to the pan,
bring to a boil, then lower the
heat and simmer for about
15 minutes.

5 Pour the soup into a warm
tureen, swirl the heavy cream
around the surface of the soup and
garnish with fresh basil leaves.
Serve immediately with croûtons.

VARIATION

*To make orange and tomato soup,
simply use half the quantity of
vegetable stock, topped up with the
same amount of fresh orange juice
and garnish the soup with
orange rind. Or to make tomato
and carrot soup, add half the
quantity again of vegetable stock
with the same amount of carrot
juice and 1¼ cups grated carrot to
the recipe, cooking the carrot with
the onion.*

Potato & Parsley Soup with Pesto

Fresh pesto is a treat to the taste buds and very different in flavor from the jars of pesto available from supermarkets.

Serves 4

INGREDIENTS

3 slices bacon
2 tbsp butter
1 pound mealy potatoes
1 pound onions
$2^{1}/_{2}$ cups chicken stock
$2^{1}/_{2}$ cups milk
$3/_{4}$ cup dried conchigliette
$5/_{8}$ cup heavy cream
chopped fresh parsley
salt and black pepper

freshly grated Parmesan cheese and garlic bread, to serve

PESTO SAUCE:
1 cup finely chopped fresh parsley
2 garlic cloves, crushed
$2/_{3}$ cup pine nuts, crushed
2 tbsp chopped fresh basil leaves

$2/_{3}$ cup freshly grated Parmesan cheese
white pepper
$5/_{8}$ cup olive oil

1 To make the pesto sauce, put all of the ingredients in a blender or food processor and process for 2 minutes, or blend together by hand (see Cook's Tip).

2 Finely chop the bacon, potatoes, and onions. Fry the bacon in a large pan over a medium heat for 4 minutes. Add the butter, potatoes, and onions and cook for 12 minutes, stirring constantly.

3 Add the stock and milk to the pan, bring to a boil, and simmer for 10 minutes. Add the conchigliette and simmer for a further 12-14 minutes.

4 Blend in the cream and simmer for 5 minutes. Add the parsley and 2 tbsp pesto sauce. Transfer the soup to serving bowls and serve with Parmesan cheese and fresh garlic bread.

COOK'S TIP

If you are making pesto by hand, it is best to use a mortar and pestle. Thoroughly grind together the parsley, garlic, pine nuts, and basil to make a paste, then mix in the cheese and pepper. Finally, gradually beat in the oil.

Ravioli alla Parmigiana

This soup is the traditional "Minestra" served at Easter and Christmas in the province of Parma.

Serves 4

INGREDIENTS

10 ounces Basic Pasta Dough
 (see page 4)
5 cups veal stock
freshly grated Parmesan cheese,
 to serve

FILLING:
1 cup freshly grated Parmesan
 cheese
1²/₃ cup fine white breadcrumbs
2 eggs

¹/₂ cup espagnole sauce (see Cook's
 Tip)
1 small onion, finely chopped
1 tsp freshly grated nutmeg

1 Make the basic pasta dough (see page 4). Carefully roll out 2 sheets of the pasta dough and cover with a damp dish cloth while you prepare the filling for the ravioli.

2 To make the filling, mix together the freshly grated Parmesan cheese, fine white breadcrumbs, eggs, espagnole sauce (see Cook's Tip), finely chopped onion, and the freshly grated nutmeg in a large mixing bowl.

3 Place spoonfuls of the filling at regular intervals on 1 sheet of pasta dough. Cover with the second sheet of pasta dough, then cut into squares and seal the edges.

4 Bring the veal stock to a boil in a large saucepan. Add the ravioli to the pan and cook for about 15 minutes.

5 Transfer the soup and ravioli to warm serving bowls and serve at once, generously sprinkled with Parmesan cheese.

COOK'S TIP

For espagnole sauce, melt 2 tbsp butter and stir in ¼ cup all-purpose flour. Cook over a low heat, stirring, until lightly colored. Add 1 tsp tomato paste, then stir in 1⅛ cups hot veal stock, 1 tbsp Madeira, and 1½ tsp white wine vinegar. Dice 1 ounce each bacon, carrot, and onion and ½ ounce each celery, leek, and fennel. Cook with a thyme sprig and a bay leaf in oil until soft. Drain, add to the sauce, and simmer for 4 hours. Strain before using.

Pea & Egg Noodle Soup with Parmesan Cheese Croûtons

This is a delicious and filling treat on cold winter evenings.

Serves 4

INGREDIENTS

3 slices bacon, diced
1 large onion, chopped
1 tbsp butter

$2^{1}/_{2}$ cups dried peas, soaked in cold
    water for 2 hours and drained
10 cups chicken stock
8 ounces dried egg noodles
$^{5}/_{8}$ cup heavy cream
salt and pepper

chopped fresh parsley, to garnish
Parmesan cheese croûtons (see
    Cook's Tip), to serve

1 Put the bacon, onion, and butter into a large saucepan and cook over a low heat for about 6 minutes.

2 Add the peas and the chicken stock to the pan and bring to a boil. Season lightly with salt and pepper, cover, and simmer for $1^{1}/_{2}$ hours.

3 Add the egg noodles to the pan and simmer for a further 15 minutes.

4 Pour in the cream and blend thoroughly. Transfer to a warm tureen, garnish with parsley, and top with Parmesan cheese croûtons (see Cook's Tip). Serve immediately.

VARIATION

Other legumes, such as dried navy beans, borlotti, or pinto beans, may be substituted for the peas in this recipe.

COOK'S TIP

To make Parmesan cheese croûtons, cut a baguette into slices. Coat each slice lightly with olive oil and sprinkle with Parmesan cheese. Broil for about 30 seconds.

Navy Bean & Pasta Soup

This soup makes an excellent winter lunch served with
warm crusty bread and a slice of cheese.

Serves 4

INGREDIENTS

$1^1/_3$ cups navy beans, soaked for
   3 hours in cold water and drained
4 tbsp olive oil
2 large onions, sliced
3 garlic cloves, chopped
14 ounce can chopped tomatoes
1 tsp dried oregano

1 tsp tomato paste
$3^1/_2$ cups water
$3/_4$ cup dried fusilli
   or conchigliette
4 ounces sun-dried tomatoes,
   drained and thinly sliced

1 tbsp chopped fresh cilantro or flat
   leaf parsley
salt and pepper
2 tbsp Parmesan cheese shavings,
   to serve

1 Put the navy beans in a large saucepan, add sufficient cold water to cover, and bring to a boil over a high heat. Boil vigorously for 15 minutes. Drain thoroughly and keep warm.

2 Heat the oil in a pan over medium heat and sauté the onions for 2–3 minutes, or until they are just beginning to change color. Stir in the garlic and cook for 1 minute. Stir in the tomatoes, oregano, and tomato paste.

3 Add the water and the reserved beans to the pan. Bring to a boil, cover, then lower the heat, and simmer for about 45 minutes, or until the beans are almost tender.

4 Add the pasta to the pan and season to taste with salt and pepper. Stir in the sun-dried tomatoes, bring back to a boil, partly cover, and simmer for 10 minutes, or until the pasta is tender, but still firm to the bite.

5 Stir the cilantro or parsley into the soup. Ladle the soup into a warm tureen, sprinkle with the Parmesan cheese shavings, and serve immediately.

COOK'S TIP

If preferred, place the beans in a pan of cold water and bring to a boil. Remove from the heat and leave the beans to cool in the water. Drain and rinse before using.

Garbanzo Bean & Chicken Soup

This hearty and nourishing soup is an ideal starter for a family supper.

Serves 4

INGREDIENTS

2 tbsp butter
3 scallions, chopped
2 garlic cloves, crushed
1 fresh marjoram sprig,
   finely chopped
12 ounces boned chicken
   breasts, diced

12 ounce can garbanzo
   beans, drained
5 cups chicken stock
1 bouquet garni
1 red bell pepper, diced
1 green bell pepper, diced

1 cup small dried pasta shapes, such
   as elbow macaroni
salt and white pepper
croûtons, to serve

1 Melt the butter in a large saucepan. Add the scallions, garlic, sprig of fresh marjoram, and the diced chicken to the saucepan and cook, stirring frequently, over a medium heat for 5 minutes.

2 Add the chicken stock, garbanzo beans, and bouquet garni to the saucepan and then season to taste with salt and white pepper.

3 Bring the soup to a boil, lower the heat, and then simmer gently for about 2 hours.

4 Add the diced bell peppers and pasta to the pan, then simmer for a further 20 minutes.

5 Transfer the soup to a warm tureen. To serve, ladle the soup into individual serving bowls and serve immediately garnished with the croûtons.

COOK'S TIP

If you prefer, you can use dried garbanzo beans. Cover with cold water and set aside to soak for 5–8 hours. Drain and add the beans to the soup, according to the recipe, and allow an additional 30 minutes–1 hour cooking time.

Cream of Lemon & Chicken Soup with Spaghetti

This delicately flavored summer soup is surprisingly easy to make.

Serves 4

INGREDIENTS

4 tbsp butter
8 shallots, thinly sliced
2 carrots, thinly sliced
2 celery stalks, thinly sliced
8 ounces boned chicken breasts,
  finely chopped

3 lemons
5 cups chicken stock
8 ounces dried spaghetti, broken into
  small pieces
$5/8$ cup heavy cream
salt and white pepper

TO GARNISH:
fresh parsley sprig
3 lemon slices, halved

---

1 Melt the butter in a large saucepan. Add the shallots, carrots, celery, and chicken and cook over a low heat, stirring occasionally, for 8 minutes.

2 Thinly pare the lemons and blanch the lemon rind in boiling water for 3 minutes. Squeeze the juice from the lemons.

3 Add the lemon rind and juice to the pan, together with the chicken stock. Slowly bring to a boil over a low heat and simmer for 40 minutes.

4 Add the spaghetti to the pan and cook for 15 minutes. Season to taste with salt and white pepper and add the cream. Heat through, but do not allow the soup to boil or it will curdle.

5 Pour the soup into a tureen or individual bowls, garnish with the parsley and half slices of lemon, and serve immediately.

COOK'S TIP

You can prepare this soup up to the end of step 3 in advance, so that all you need do before serving is heat it through before adding the pasta and the finishing touches.

Chicken & Corn Soup

This heartwarming soup is both quick and easy to make.

Serves 4

INGREDIENTS

1 pound boned chicken breasts, cut into strips

5 cups chicken stock

$^5/_8$ cup heavy cream

$^3/_4$ cup dried vermicelli

1 tbsp cornstarch

3 tbsp milk

6 ounces corn kernels

salt and pepper

1 Put the chicken, stock, and cream into a large saucepan and bring to a boil over a low heat. Reduce the heat slightly and simmer for about 20 minutes. Season the soup with salt and black pepper to taste.

2 Meanwhile, cook the vermicelli in lightly salted boiling water for 10-12 minutes, until just tender. Drain the pasta and keep warm.

3 In a small bowl, mix together the cornstarch and milk to make a smooth paste. Stir the

cornstarch paste into the soup until thickened.

4 Add the corn and vermicelli to the saucepan and heat through.

5 Transfer the soup to a warm tureen or individual soup bowls and serve immediately.

COOK'S TIP

If you are short of time, buy ready-cooked chicken, remove any skin, and cut it into slices.

VARIATION

For crab and corn soup, substitute 1 pound cooked crabmeat for the chicken breasts. Flake the crabmeat thoroughly before adding it to the saucepan and reduce the cooking time by 10 minutes. For a Chinese-style soup, substitute egg noodles for the vermicelli and use canned, creamed corn.

Veal & Ham Soup with Sherry

Veal and ham is a classic combination, used here to good effect to create a richly flavored Italian soup.

Serves 4

INGREDIENTS

4 tbsp butter
1 onion, diced
1 carrot, diced
1 celery stalk, diced
1 pound very thinly sliced veal
1 pound thinly sliced ham

$1/2$ cup all-purpose flour
$4^{3}/8$ cups beef stock
1 bay leaf
8 black peppercorns
pinch of salt
3 tbsp redcurrant jelly

$5/8$ cup cream sherry
$3/4$ cup dried vermicelli
garlic croûtons, to serve

1 Melt the butter in a large saucepan. Add the onions, carrot, celery, veal, and ham and cook over a low heat for about 6 minutes.

2 Sprinkle in the flour and cook, stirring constantly, for a further 2 minutes. Gradually stir in the stock, then add the bay leaf, peppercorns, and salt. Bring to a boil and simmer for 1 hour.

3 Remove the pan from the heat and add the redcurrant jelly and cream sherry. Set aside for about 4 hours.

4 Remove the bay leaf from the pan and discard. Reheat the soup over a very low heat until warmed through.

5 Meanwhile, cook the vermicelli in a saucepan of lightly salted boiling water for 10-12 minutes. Stir the vermicelli into the soup and transfer to warm soup bowls. Serve with garlic croûtons (see Cook's Tip).

COOK'S TIP

To make garlic croûtons, remove the crusts from 3 slices of day-old white bread. Cut the bread into ¼ inch cubes. Heat 3 tbsp olive oil over a low heat and stir-fry 1–2 finely chopped garlic cloves for 1–2 minutes. Remove the garlic and add the bread. Cook, tossing the pan and stirring frequently, until golden brown. Remove from the pan with a slotted spoon and drain on paper towels.

Tuscan Veal Broth

Veal plays an important role in Italian cuisine and there are dozens of recipes for all cuts of this meat. Prepare this recipe well in advance.

Serves 4

INGREDIENTS

$1/3$ cup dried peas, soaked for 2 hours and drained

2 pounds boned neck of veal, diced

5 cups beef or brown stock (see Cook's Tip)

$2^1/2$ cups water

$1/3$ cup barley, washed

1 large carrot, diced

1 small turnip (about 6 ounces), diced

1 large leek, thinly sliced

1 red onion, finely chopped

$3^1/2$ ounces chopped tomatoes

1 fresh basil sprig

$3/4$ cup dried vermicelli

salt and white pepper

1 Put the peas, veal, stock, and water into a large saucepan and bring to a boil over a low heat. Using a slotted spoon, skim off any scum that rises to the surface of the liquid.

2 When all of the scum has been removed, add the barley and a pinch of salt to the mixture. Simmer gently over a low heat for 25 minutes.

3 Add the carrot, turnip, leek, onion, tomatoes, and basil to the pan, and season with salt and pepper to taste. Simmer for about 2 hours, skimming the surface with a slotted spoon, from time to time. Remove the pan from the heat and set aside for 2 hours.

4 Set the pan over a medium heat and bring to a boil. Add the vermicelli and cook for 12 minutes. Season with salt and pepper to taste and remove and discard the basil. Ladle the soup into warm bowls and serve immediately.

COOK'S TIP

The best brown stock is made with veal bones and shin of beef roasted with drippings in the oven for 40 minutes. Transfer the bones to a large pan and add sliced leeks, onion, celery, and carrots, a bouquet garni, white wine vinegar, and a thyme sprig, and cover with cold water. Simmer over a very low heat for about 3 hours. Strain and blot the fat from the surface of the stock with paper towels.

Veal & Mushroom Soup with Vermicelli

Exotic mushrooms are available commercially and an increasing range of cultivated varieties is now to be found in many supermarkets.

Serves 4

INGREDIENTS

1 pound veal, thinly sliced

1 pound veal bones

5 cups water

1 small onion

6 peppercorns

1 tsp cloves

pinch of mace

5 ounces oyster and shiitake mushrooms, roughly chopped

$^5/_8$ cup heavy cream

$^3/_4$ cup dried vermicelli

1 tbsp cornstarch

3 tbsp milk

salt and pepper

1 Put the veal, bones, and water into a large saucepan. Bring to a boil and lower the heat. Add the onion, peppercorns, cloves, and mace and simmer for about 3 hours, until the veal stock is reduced by one-third.

2 Strain the stock, skim off any fat on the surface with a slotted spoon, and pour the stock into a clean saucepan. Add the veal meat to the pan.

3 Add the mushrooms and cream, bring to a boil over a low heat, and simmer for 12 minutes. Meanwhile, cook the vermicelli in lightly salted boiling water until tender, but still firm to the bite. Drain and keep warm.

4 Mix together the cornstarch and milk to form a smooth paste. Stir the cornstarch paste into the soup to thicken. Season to taste with salt and pepper and just before serving, add the vermicelli. Transfer the soup to a warm tureen and serve immediately.

COOK'S TIP

You can make this soup with the more inexpensive cuts of veal, such as breast or neck slices. These are lean and the long cooking time ensures that the meat is really tender.

Mussel & Potato Soup

*This quick and easy soup would make a delicious
summer lunch served with fresh crusty bread.*

Serves 4

INGREDIENTS

1 pound 10 ounces mussels
2 tbsp olive oil
7 tbsp unsalted butter
2 slices bacon, chopped
1 onion, chopped
2 garlic cloves, crushed
$^1/_2$ cup all-purpose flour

1 pound potatoes, thinly sliced
$^3/_4$ cup dried conchigliette
$1^1/_4$ cups heavy cream
1 tbsp lemon juice
2 egg yolks
salt and pepper

TO GARNISH:
2 tbsp finely chopped fresh parsley
lemon wedges

1 Debeard the mussels and scrub them under cold water for 5 minutes. Discard any mussels that do not close immediately when sharply tapped.

2 Bring a large pan of water to a boil, add the mussels, oil, and a little pepper and cook until the mussels open.

3 Drain the mussels, reserving the cooking liquid. Discard any mussels that are closed. Remove the mussels from their shells.

4 Melt the butter in a large saucepan, add the bacon, onion, and garlic and cook for 4 minutes. Carefully stir in the flour. Measure 5 cups of the reserved cooking liquid and stir it into the pan.

5 Add the potatoes to the pan and simmer for 5 minutes. Add the conchigliette and simmer for a further 10 minutes.

6 Add the cream and lemon juice, season to taste with salt and pepper, then add the mussels to the pan.

7 Blend the egg yolks with 1-2 tbsp of the remaining cooking liquid, stir into the pan, and cook for 4 minutes.

8 Ladle the soup into 4 warm individual soup bowls, garnish with the chopped fresh parsley and lemon wedges, and serve immediately.

Italian Fish Soup

This colorful mixed seafood soup would be superbly complemented by a dry white wine.

Serves 4

INGREDIENTS

4 tbsp butter
1 pound assorted fish fillets, such as
  red mullet and snapper
1 pound prepared seafood, such as
  squid and shrimp
8 ounces fresh crabmeat
1 large onion, sliced

$^1/_4$ cup all-purpose flour
5 cups fish stock (see Cook's Tip)
$^3/_4$ cup dried pasta shapes, such as
  ditalini or elbow macaroni
1 tbsp anchovy extract
grated rind and juice of 1 orange
$^1/_4$ cup dry sherry

1$^1/_4$ cups heavy cream
salt and black pepper
crusty brown bread, to serve

1 Melt the butter in a large saucepan, add the fish fillets, seafood, crabmeat, and onion, and cook gently over a low heat for 6 minutes.

2 Add the flour to the mixture, stirring thoroughly to avoid any lumps.

3 Gradually add the fish stock, stirring constantly, until the soup comes to a boil. Reduce the heat and simmer for 30 minutes.

4 Add the pasta to the saucepan and cook for a further 10 minutes.

5 Stir in the anchovy extract, orange rind, orange juice, sherry, and heavy cream. Season to taste with salt and pepper.

6 Heat the soup until completely warmed through. Transfer the soup to a tureen or to warm soup bowls and serve with crusty brown bread.

COOK'S TIP

The heads, tails, trimmings and bones of virtually any non-oily fish can be used to make fish stock. Simmer 2 pounds fish pieces, including heads, in a large saucepan with ⅝ cup white wine, 1 chopped onion, 1 sliced carrot, 1 sliced celery stalk, 4 black peppercorns, 1 bouquet garni, and 7½ cups water for 30 minutes, then strain.

Spaghetti alla Carbonara

Ensure that all of the cooked ingredients are as hot as possible
before adding the eggs, so that they cook on contact.

Serves 4

INGREDIENTS

15 ounces dried spaghetti
2 tbsp olive oil
1 large onion, thinly sliced
2 garlic cloves, chopped
6 slices bacon

2 tbsp butter
6 ounces mushrooms, thinly sliced
1¼ cups heavy cream
3 eggs, beaten

1 cup freshly grated Parmesan
cheese, plus extra to serve
(optional)
salt and pepper
fresh sage sprigs, to garnish

1 Warm a large serving dish or bowl. Bring a large pan of lightly salted water to a boil. Add the spaghetti and 1 tbsp of the oil and cook until tender, but still firm to the bite. Drain, return to the pan, and keep warm.

2 Meanwhile, heat the remaining oil in a skillet over a medium heat. Add the onion and sauté until it is transparent. Add the garlic and bacon and fry until the bacon is crisp. Transfer to the warm plate.

3 Melt the butter in the skillet. Add the mushrooms and sauté, stirring occasionally, for 3-4 minutes. Return the bacon mixture to the pan. Cover and keep warm.

4 Mix together the cream, eggs, and cheese in a large bowl and then season to taste with salt and pepper.

5 Working very quickly, tip the spaghetti into the bacon and mushroom mixture and pour in the eggs. Toss the spaghetti quickly into the egg and cream mixture, using 2 forks, and serve immediately. If you wish, serve with extra grated Parmesan cheese.

COOK'S TIP

The key to success with this recipe is not to overcook the egg. That is why it is important to keep all the ingredients hot enough just to cook the egg and to work rapidly to avoid scrambling it.

Smoked Ham Linguini

*Served with freshly made Italian bread or tossed with
pesto, this makes a mouthwatering light lunch.*

Serves 4

INGREDIENTS

1 pound dried linguini
1 pound broccoli, broken into
   florets

8 ounces Italian smoked ham
⅝ cup Italian cheese sauce (see
   Cook's Tip)

salt and pepper
Italian bread, to serve

1 Bring a large pan of lightly salted water to a boil. Add the linguini and broccoli florets and cook for 10 minutes, until the linguini is tender, but still firm to the bite.

2 Drain the linguini and broccoli thoroughly, set aside, and keep warm.

3 Meanwhile, make the Italian cheese sauce (see Cook's Tip, right).

4 Cut the Italian smoked ham into thin strips. Toss the linguini, broccoli, and ham into

the Italian cheese sauce and gently warm through over a very low heat.

5 Transfer the pasta mixture to a warm serving dish. Sprinkle with black pepper and serve with Italian bread.

COOK'S TIP

There are many types of Italian bread which would be suitable to serve with this dish. Ciabatta is made with olive oil and is available plain and with different ingredients, such as olives or sun-dried tomatoes.

COOK'S TIP

For Italian cheese sauce, melt 2 tbsp butter in a pan and stir in ¼ cup all-purpose flour. Cook, stirring, over a low heat until the roux is light in color and crumbly in texture. Stir in 1¼ cups hot milk. Cook, stirring, for 15 minutes until thick and smooth. Add a pinch of nutmeg, a pinch of dried thyme, 2 tbsp white wine vinegar, and season to taste. Stir in 3 tbsp heavy cream and mix. Stir in ½ cup grated Mozzarella cheese, ⅔ cup grated Parmesan cheese, 1 tsp English mustard, and 2 tbsp sour cream.

Chorizo & Mushrooms with a Spicy Vermicelli

Simple and quick to make, this spicy dish will set the taste buds tingling.

Serves 6

INGREDIENTS

1¹/₂ pounds dried vermicelli
¹/₂ cup olive oil
2 garlic cloves
4¹/₂ ounces chorizo, sliced

8 ounces exotic mushrooms
3 fresh red chilies, chopped
2 tbsp freshly grated
   Parmesan cheese

salt and pepper
10 anchovy fillets, to garnish

1 Bring a large saucepan of lightly salted water to a boil. Add the vermicelli and 1 tablespoon of the oil and cook until just tender, but still firm to the bite. Drain, place on a large, warm serving plate and keep warm until required.

2 Meanwhile heat the remaining oil in a large skillet. Add the garlic and fry for 1 minute. Add the chorizo and mushrooms and cook for about 4 minutes, then add the chopped chilies, and cook for 1 minute.

3 Pour the chorizo and mushroom mixture over the vermicelli and season with a little salt and pepper. Sprinkle with freshly grated Parmesan cheese, garnish with a lattice of anchovy fillets, and serve immediately.

VARIATION

Fresh sardines may be used in this recipe in place of the chorizo. However, ensure that you gut and clean the sardines, removing the backbone, before using them.

COOK'S TIP

Always obtain exotic mushrooms from a reliable source and never pick them yourself. Mixed color oyster mushrooms have been used here, but you could also use chanterelles. However, remember that chanterelles tend to shrink during cooking, so you may need a larger quantity.

Pancetta & Pecorino Cakes on a Bed of Farfalle

This makes an excellent starter served with a topping of pesto or anchovy sauce.

Serves 4

INGREDIENTS

2 tbsp butter, plus extra
  for greasing
3^1/$_2$ ounces pancetta, rind removed
2 cups self-rising flour
^{7}/$_8$ cup grated pecorino cheese

^{5}/$_8$ cup milk, plus extra for glazing
1 tbsp ketchup
1 tsp Worcestershire sauce
3^1/$_2$ cups dried farfalle
1 tbsp olive oil

salt and black pepper
3 tbsp pesto (see page 12) or
  anchovy sauce (optional)
salad greens, to serve

1 Grease a cookie sheet with a little butter. Broil the pancetta until it is cooked. Allow the pancetta to cool, then chop it finely.

2 Sift together the flour and a pinch of salt into a mixing bowl. Add the butter and rub in with your fingertips. When the butter and flour have been thoroughly incorporated, add the pancetta and one-third of the grated cheese.

3 Mix together the milk, ketchup, and Worcestershire sauce and add to the dry ingredients, mixing to make a soft dough.

4 Roll out the dough on a lightly floured board to make a 7-inch round. Brush with a little milk to glaze and cut into 8 wedges.

5 Arrange the dough wedges on the prepared cookie sheet and sprinkle with the remaining cheese. Bake in a preheated oven at 400°F for 20 minutes.

6 Meanwhile, bring a saucepan of lightly salted water to a boil. Add the farfalle and the oil and cook until just tender, but still firm to the bite. Drain thoroughly and transfer to a large serving dish. Top with the pancetta and pecorino cakes. Serve with the sauce of your choice and salad greens.

Orecchiette with Bacon & Tomatoes

As this dish cooks, the mouthwatering aroma of
bacon, sweet tomatoes, and oregano is a feast in itself.

Serves 4

INGREDIENTS

2 pounds small, sweet tomatoes
6 slices smoked bacon
4 tbsp butter
1 onion, chopped

1 garlic clove, crushed
4 fresh oregano sprigs,
   finely chopped
4 cups dried orecchiette

1 tbsp olive oil
salt and pepper
freshly grated Pecorino cheese,
   to serve

1 Blanch the tomatoes in boiling water. Drain, skin, and seed the tomatoes, then roughly chop the flesh. Chop the bacon into small pieces.

2 Melt the butter in a saucepan. Add the bacon and fry until it is golden. Add the onion and garlic and fry over a medium heat for 5-7 minutes, until softened.

3 Add the tomatoes and oregano to the saucepan and season to taste with salt and pepper. Lower the heat and simmer for 10-12 minutes.

4 Bring a large pan of lightly salted water to a boil. Add the orecchiette and oil and cook for 12 minutes, until just tender, but still firm to the bite. Drain the pasta and transfer to a warm serving dish. Spoon the bacon and tomato sauce over the pasta, toss to coat, and serve with the cheese.

VARIATION

You could also use 1 pound spicy Italian sausages. Squeeze the meat out of the skins and add to the pan in step 2 instead of the bacon.

COOK'S TIP

For an authentic Italian flavor use pancetta, rather than ordinary bacon. This kind of bacon is streaked with fat and adds rich undertones of flavor to many traditional dishes. It is available both smoked and unsmoked, and can be bought in a single, large piece or cut into slices. You can buy it in some supermarkets and all Italian delicatessens.

Creamed Veal Kidneys with Penne & Pesto Sauce

Veal kidneys have a wonderfully rich flavor, but they are quite delicate and should never be overcooked.

Serves 4

INGREDIENTS

5 tbsp butter

12 veal kidneys, trimmed and thinly sliced

6 ounces button mushrooms, sliced

1 tsp English mustard

pinch of freshly grated ginger root

2 tbsp dry sherry

$5/8$ cup heavy cream

2 tbsp pesto sauce (see page 12)

14 ounces dried penne

1 tbsp olive oil

salt and pepper

4 slices of hot toast cut into triangles

fresh parsley sprigs, to garnish

1 Melt the butter in a large skillet. Add the kidneys and fry over a low heat for 4 minutes. With a slotted spoon transfer the kidneys to an ovenproof dish and keep warm.

2 Add the mushrooms to the skillet, and cook for about 2 minutes.

3 Add the mustard and ginger to the pan and season to taste with salt and pepper. Cook for

2 minutes, then add the sherry, cream, and pesto sauce. Cook for a further 3 minutes, then pour the sauce over the kidneys. Bake in a preheated oven at 375°F for 10 minutes.

4 Meanwhile, bring a large pan of lightly salted water to a boil. Add the penne and the oil and cook until just tender, but still firm to the bite. Drain the pasta thoroughly and transfer to a warm serving dish.

5 Top the pasta with the kidneys in the pesto sauce. Place triangles of warm toast around the kidneys, garnish with fresh parsley sprigs, and serve immediately.

COOK'S TIP

Store the pesto sauce in an airtight container for up to a week in the refrigerator, or freeze (without adding the Parmesan cheese) for several months.

Marinated Eggplant on a Bed of Linguine

This unusual, fruity marinade makes the eggplant slices simply melt in the mouth.

Serves 4

INGREDIENTS

⅝ cup vegetable stock
⅝ cup white wine vinegar
2 tsp balsamic vinegar
3 tbsp olive oil
fresh oregano sprig

1 pound eggplant, peeled and
   thinly sliced
14 ounces dried linguine

MARINADE:
2 tbsp extra virgin oil
2 garlic cloves, crushed

2 tbsp chopped fresh oregano
2 tbsp finely chopped
   roasted almonds
2 tbsp diced red bell pepper
2 tbsp lime juice
grated rind and juice of 1 orange
salt and pepper

1 Put the vegetable stock, wine vinegar, and balsamic vinegar into a saucepan and bring to a boil over a low heat. Add 2 tsp of the olive oil and the sprig of oregano and simmer gently for about 1 minute.

2 Add the eggplant slices to the saucepan, remove from the heat and set aside for about 10 minutes.

3 Meanwhile make the marinade. Combine the olive oil, garlic, fresh oregano, almonds, bell pepper, lime juice, orange rind, and juice in a large bowl and season to taste with salt and pepper.

4 Carefully remove the eggplant from the saucepan with a slotted spoon, and drain well. Add the eggplant slices to the marinade,

mixing well, and set aside in the refrigerator for about 12 hours.

5 Bring a large pan of lightly salted water to a boil. Add half the remaining oil and the linguine and cook until just tender. Drain the pasta and toss with the remaining oil while still warm. Arrange the pasta on a serving plate with the eggplant slices and the marinade and serve.

Spinach & Ricotta Shells

This is a classic combination in which the smooth, creamy
cheese balances the sharper taste of the spinach.

Serves 4

INGREDIENTS

14 ounces dried lumache
  rigate grande
5 tbsp olive oil
1 cup fresh white breadcrumbs
$^1/_2$ cup milk

$10^1/_2$ ounces frozen spinach, thawed
  and drained
1 cup ricotta cheese
pinch of freshly grated nutmeg

14 ounce can chopped tomatoes,
  drained
1 garlic clove, crushed
salt and pepper

1 Bring a large saucepan of lightly salted water to a boil. Add the lumache and 1 tbsp of the olive oil and cook until just tender, but still firm to the bite. Drain the pasta, rinse under cold water, and set aside.

2 Put the breadcrumbs, milk, and 3 tbsp of the remaining olive oil in a food processor and work to combine.

3 Add the spinach and ricotta cheese to the food processor and work to a smooth mixture.

Transfer to a bowl, stir in the nutmeg, and season with salt and pepper to taste.

4 Mix together the tomatoes, garlic, and remaining oil and spoon the mixture into the base of an ovenproof dish.

5 Using a teaspoon, fill the lumache with the spinach and ricotta mixture and arrange on top of the tomato mixture in the dish. Cover and bake in a preheated oven at 350°F for 20 minutes. Serve hot.

COOK'S TIP

Ricotta is a creamy Italian cheese traditionally made from ewes' milk whey. It is soft and white, with a smooth texture and a slightly sweet flavor. It should be used within 2–3 days of purchase.

Rotelle with Spicy Italian Sauce

This filling vegetarian dish is perfect for an inexpensive and quick lunch.

Serves 4

INGREDIENTS

5 tbsp olive oil
3 garlic cloves, crushed
2 fresh red chilies, chopped

1 green chili, chopped
2⁷/₈ cup Italian red wine sauce (see Cook's Tip, bottom right)

3¹/₂ cups dried rotelle
salt and pepper
warm Italian bread, to serve

1 Make the Italian Red Wine Sauce (see Cook's Tip, right).

2 Heat 4 tbsp of the oil in a saucepan. Add the garlic and chilies and sauté for 3 minutes.

3 Stir in the Italian red wine sauce, season with a little salt and pepper to taste, and simmer gently over a low heat for about 20 minutes.

4 Bring a large saucepan of lightly salted water to a boil. Add the rotelle and the remaining oil and cook for 8 minutes, until just tender, but still firm to the bite. Drain the pasta.

5 Toss the rotelle in the spicy sauce, transfer to a warm serving dish, and serve with warm Italian bread.

COOK'S TIP

Take care when using fresh chilies as they can burn your skin. Handle them as little as possible—wear rubber gloves if necessary. Always wash your hands thoroughly afterward, and don't touch your face or eyes before you have washed your hands. Remove chili seeds before chopping the chilies, as they are the hottest part, and shouldn't be allowed to slip into the food.

COOK'S TIP

To make Italian red wine sauce, first make a demi-glace sauce by combining ⅝ cup each brown stock (see page 28) and espagnole sauce (see page 14), cook for 10 minutes, and strain. Meanwhile, combine ½ cup red wine, 2 tbsp red wine vinegar, 4 tbsp chopped shallots, 1 bay leaf and 1 thyme sprig in a small saucepan. Bring to a boil and allow to reduce by about three-quarters. Add the demi-glace sauce to the pan and simmer for about 20 minutes. Season with a little pepper taste and strain before using.

Tricolor Timballini

*An unusual way of serving pasta, these cheese molds
are excellent with a crunchy salad for a light lunch.*

Serves 4

INGREDIENTS

1 tbsp butter, softened
1 cup dried white breadcrumbs
6 ounces dried tricolor spaghetti,
    broken into 2-inch lengths
3 tbsp olive oil
1 egg yolk

1 cup grated Swiss cheese
1¼ cups béchamel sauce (see
    page 166)
1 onion, finely chopped
1 bay leaf
⅝ cup dry white wine

⅝ cup sieved tomatoes
1 tbsp tomato paste
salt and pepper
fresh basil leaves, to garnish

1 Grease four ¾ cup molds or ramekins with the butter. Evenly coat the insides with half the breadcrumbs.

2 Bring a saucepan of lightly salted water to a boil. Add the spaghetti and 1 tbsp of the oil and cook until just tender. Drain and transfer to a mixing bowl.

3 Add the egg yolk and cheese to the pasta and season. Pour the béchamel sauce into the bowl and mix. Spoon the mixture into the ramekins and sprinkle with the remaining breadcrumbs.

4 Stand the ramekins on a cookie sheet and bake in a preheated oven at 425°F for 20 minutes. Set aside for 10 minutes.

5 Meanwhile, make the sauce. Heat the remaining oil in a pan and gently sauté the onion and bay leaf for 2-3 minutes.

6 Stir in the wine, sieved tomatoes, and tomato paste and season. Simmer for 20 minutes, until thickened. Remove and discard the bay leaf.

7 Turn the timballini out onto individual serving plates, garnish with the basil leaves, and serve with the tomato sauce.

Tagliarini with Gorgonzola

This simple, creamy pasta sauce is a classic Italian recipe.

Serves 4

INGREDIENTS

2 tbsp butter
8 ounces Gorgonzola cheese,
  roughly crumbled
5/8 cup heavy cream

2 tbsp dry white wine
1 tsp cornstarch
4 fresh sage sprigs, finely chopped
14 ounces dried tagliarini

2 tbsp olive oil
salt and white pepper

1 Melt the butter in a heavy-based saucepan. Stir in 6 ounces of the Gorgonzola cheese and melt, over a low heat, for about 2 minutes.

2 Add the cream, wine, and cornstarch to the pan and beat with a whisk until fully incorporated.

3 Stir in the sage and season to taste with salt and white pepper. Bring to a boil over a low heat, whisking constantly, until the sauce thickens. Remove from the heat and set aside while you cook the pasta.

4 Bring a large saucepan of lightly salted water to a boil. Add the tagliarini and 1 tbsp of the olive oil. Cook the pasta for 12–14 minutes, or until just tender, drain thoroughly, and toss in the remaining olive oil. Transfer the pasta to a serving dish and keep warm.

5 Return the saucepan containing the sauce to a low heat to reheat the sauce, whisking constantly. Spoon the Gorgonzola sauce over the tagliarini, generously sprinkle with the remaining crumbled cheese, and serve immediately.

COOK'S TIP

Gorgonzola is one of the world's oldest veined cheeses and, arguably, its finest. When buying, always check that it is creamy yellow with delicate green veining. Avoid hard or discolored cheese. It should have a rich, piquant aroma, not a bitter smell. If you find Gorgonzola too strong or rich, you could substitute a milder blue cheese.

Gnocchi Piemontese

Gnocchi, a speciality from northern Italy, are small dumplings that are either poached or baked.

Serves 4

INGREDIENTS

1 pound warm mashed potato
⁵/₈ cup self-rising flour
1 egg
2 egg yolks

1 tbsp olive oil
⁵/₈ cup espagnole sauce (see page 14)
4 tbsp butter

2 cups freshly grated Parmesan cheese
salt and pepper

---

1 In a large bowl, mix together the mashed potato and flour. Add the egg and egg yolks, season well with salt and pepper, and mix together to form a dough.

2 Break off pieces of the dough and roll them between the palms of your hands to form small balls the size of a walnut. Flatten the balls with a fork into the shape of small circles.

3 Bring a large pan of lightly salted water to a boil. Add the gnocchi and olive oil and poach for 10 minutes.

4 Mix the espagnole sauce (see page 14) and the butter in a large saucepan over a gentle heat. Gradually blend in the grated Parmesan cheese.

5 Remove the gnocchi from the pan with a slotted spoon. Toss the gnocchi in the sauce, transfer to 4 individual serving plates, and serve immediately.

COOK'S TIP

This dish also makes an excellent main meal with a crisp salad.

VARIATION

These gnocchi would also taste delicious with a tomato sauce, in Trentino-style. Mix together 1 cup finely chopped sun-dried tomatoes, 1 finely sliced celery stalk, 1 crushed garlic clove, and 6 tbsp red wine in a pan. Cook over a low heat for 15–20 minutes. Stir in 8 skinned, chopped, Italian plum tomatoes, season to taste with salt and pepper, and simmer over a low heat for a further 10 minutes.

Pasta Omelet

This is a superb way of using up any leftover pasta,
such as penne, macaroni, or conchiglie.

Serves 2

INGREDIENTS

4 tbsp olive oil
1 small onion, chopped
1 fennel bulb, thinly sliced
4$\frac{1}{2}$ ounces potato, diced
1 garlic clove, chopped

4 eggs
1 tbsp chopped fresh parsley
pinch of chili powder
3$\frac{1}{2}$ ounces cooked short pasta
2 tbsp stuffed green olives, halved

salt and pepper
fresh marjoram sprigs, to garnish
tomato salad, to serve

1 Heat half the oil in a heavy-based skillet over a low heat. Add the onion, fennel, and potato and cook, stirring occasionally, for 8-10 minutes, until the potato is just tender.

2 Stir in the garlic and cook for 1 minute. Remove the pan from the heat, transfer the vegetables to a plate, and set aside.

3 Beat the eggs until they are frothy. Stir in the parsley and season with salt, pepper, and a pinch of chili powder.

4 Heat 1 tablespoon of the remaining oil in a clean skillet. Add half of the egg mixture to the pan, then add the cooked vegetables, pasta, and half of the olives. Pour in the remaining egg mixture and cook until the sides begin to set.

5 Lift up the edges of the omelette with a spatula to allow the uncooked egg to spread underneath. Cook, shaking the pan occasionally, until the underside of the omelet is a light golden brown color.

6 Slide the omelet out of the pan onto a plate. Wipe the pan with paper towels and heat the remaining oil. Invert the omelet into the pan and cook until the other side is golden brown.

7 Slide the omelet onto a warmed serving dish and garnish with the remaining olives and the marjoram. Serve cut into wedges, with a tomato salad.

Spaghetti with Ricotta Cheese

This light pasta dish has a delicate flavor
ideally suited to a summer lunch.

Serves 4

INGREDIENTS

12 ounces dried spaghetti
3 tbsp olive oil
3 tbsp butter
2 tbsp chopped fresh parsley
1 cup freshly ground almonds

$^1/_2$ cup ricotta cheese
pinch of grated nutmeg
pinch of ground cinnamon
$^5/_8$ cup unsweetened yogurt
$^1/_2$ cup hot chicken stock

1 tbsp pine nuts
salt and pepper
fresh parsley sprigs, to garnish

---

1 Bring a large pan of lightly salted water to a boil. Add the spaghetti and 1 tbsp of the oil and cook until tender, but still firm to the bite.

2 Drain the pasta, return to the pan, and toss with the butter and chopped parsley. Set aside and keep warm.

3 To make the sauce, mix together the ground almonds, ricotta cheese, nutmeg, cinnamon, and unsweetened yogurt over a low heat to form a thick paste. Gradually stir in the remaining oil. When the oil has been fully incorporated, gradually stir in the hot chicken stock, until smooth. Season the sauce with black pepper to taste.

4 Transfer the spaghetti to a warm serving dish, pour the sauce on top, and toss together well (see Cook's Tip). Sprinkle with the pine nuts, garnish with the fresh parsley, and serve the spaghetti warm.

COOK'S TIP

Use two large forks to toss spaghetti or other long pasta, so that it is thoroughly coated with the sauce. Special spaghetti forks are available from some cookware departments and kitchen stores. Holding one fork in each hand, gently ease the prongs under the pasta on each side and lift them toward the center. Continue this evenly and rhythmically until the pasta is completely coated.

Gnocchi Romana

This is a traditional recipe but, for a less rich version, omit the eggs.

Serves 4

INGREDIENTS

3$\frac{1}{8}$ cups milk
pinch of freshly grated nutmeg
6 tbsp butter, plus extra
   for greasing

1$\frac{1}{4}$ cups cream of wheat
1$\frac{1}{2}$ cups grated Parmesan cheese
2 eggs, beaten
$\frac{1}{2}$ cup grated Swiss cheese

salt and pepper
fresh basil sprigs, to garnish

1 Pour the milk into a saucepan and bring to a boil. Remove the pan from the heat and stir in the nutmeg, 2 tbsp of the butter, and salt and pepper to taste.

2 Gradually stir the semolina into the milk, whisking to prevent lumps forming, and return the pan to a low heat. Simmer, stirring constantly, for about 10 minutes, until the mixture is very thick.

3 Beat $\frac{2}{3}$ cup of Parmesan cheese into the semolina mixture, then beat in the eggs. Continue beating the mixture

until it is smooth. Set the mixture aside for a few minutes to cool slightly.

4 Spread out the semolina mixture in an even layer on a sheet of waxed paper or in a large, oiled baking pan, smoothing the surface with a damp spatula—it should be about $\frac{1}{2}$-inch thick. Set aside to cool completely, then leave to chill in the refrigerator for 1 hour.

5 Once chilled, cut out rounds of gnocchi, measuring about 1$\frac{1}{2}$ inches in diameter, using a plain, greased pastry cutter.

6 Grease a shallow ovenproof dish or 4 individual dishes. Lay the gnocchi trimmings in the base of the dish or dishes and cover with overlapping rounds of gnocchi.

7 Melt the remaining butter and drizzle over the gnocchi. Sprinkle with the remaining Parmesan cheese and the Swiss cheese.

8 Bake in a preheated oven at 400°F for 25-30 minutes, until the top is crisp and golden brown. Serve hot, garnished with the basil.

Three Cheese Bake

*Serve this dish while the cheese is still hot and melted, as cooked
cheese turns very rubbery if it is allowed to cool down.*

Serves 4

INGREDIENTS

butter, for greasing
14 ounces dried penne
1 tbsp olive oil
2 eggs, beaten

1¹/₂ cups ricotta cheese
4 fresh basil sprigs
1 cup grated mozzarella or
halloumi cheese

4 tbsp freshly grated
Parmesan cheese
salt and black pepper
fresh basil leaves (optional), to garnish

1 Lightly grease an ovenproof
dish with butter.

2 Bring a large pan of lightly
salted water to a boil. Add the
penne and olive oil and cook until
just tender, but still firm to the
bite. Drain the pasta, set aside, and
keep warm.

3 Beat the eggs into the ricotta
cheese and season to taste
with salt and pepper.

4 Spoon half of the penne into
the base of the dish and cover
with half of the basil leaves.

5 Spoon over half of the ricotta
cheese mixture. Sprinkle with
the mozzarella or halloumi cheese
and then top with the remaining
basil leaves. Cover with the
remaining penne and then spoon
over the remaining ricotta cheese
mixture. Lightly sprinkle with the
grated Parmesan cheese.

6 Bake in a preheated oven at
375°F for 30–40 minutes,
until golden brown and the cheese
topping is hot and bubbling.

7 Garnish with basil leaves, if
desired, and serve hot.

VARIATION

*Try substituting smoked Bavarian
cheese for the mozzarella or
halloumi and grated Cheddar
cheese for the Parmesan, for a
slightly different but just as
delicious flavor.*

Baked Rigatoni Filled with Tuna & Ricotta Cheese

Ribbed tubes of pasta are filled with fish and cheese and then baked in a creamy sauce.

Serves 4

INGREDIENTS

butter, for greasing
1 pound dried rigatoni
1 tbsp olive oil
7 ounce can flaked tuna, drained

1 cup ricotta cheese
$^1/_2$ cup heavy cream
$2^2/_3$ cups grated Parmesan cheese

4 ounces sun-dried tomatoes, drained and sliced
salt and black pepper

1 Lightly grease an ovenproof dish with butter.

2 Bring a large saucepan of lightly salted water to a boil. Add the rigatoni and olive oil and cook until just tender, but still firm to the bite. Drain the pasta and set aside until cool enough to handle.

3 In a bowl, mix together the tuna and ricotta cheese to form a soft paste. Spoon the mixture into a piping bag and use to fill the rigatoni. Arrange the filled pasta tubes side by side in the prepared ovenproof dish.

4 To make the sauce, mix the cream and Parmesan cheese, and season. Spoon the sauce over the rigatoni and top with the sun-dried tomatoes arranged in a criss-cross pattern. Bake in a preheated oven at 400°F for 20 minutes. Serve immediately straight from the dish.

VARIATION

For a vegetarian alternative of this recipe, simply substitute a mixture of pitted and chopped black olives and chopped walnuts for the tuna. Follow exactly the same cooking method.

Spaghetti with Anchovy & Pesto Sauce

This is an ideal dish for cooks in a hurry and for those who do not have much time for shopping, as it is prepared in minutes from cupboard ingredients.

Serves 4

INGREDIENTS

³/₈ cup olive oil
2 garlic cloves, crushed
2 ounce can anchovy fillets, drained
1 pound dried spaghetti

2 ounces pesto sauce (see page 12)
2 tbsp finely chopped fresh oregano
1 cup grated Parmesan cheese, plus
  extra for serving (optional)

salt and pepper
2 fresh oregano sprigs, to garnish

1 Reserve 1 tbsp of the oil and heat the remainder in a small saucepan. Add the garlic and fry for 3 minutes.

2 Lower the heat, stir in the anchovies, and cook, stirring occasionally, until the anchovies have disintegrated.

3 Bring a large saucepan of lightly salted water to a boil. Add the spaghetti and the remaining olive oil and cook until just tender, but still firm to the bite.

4 Add the pesto sauce (see page 12) and chopped fresh oregano to the anchovy mixture and then season with black pepper to taste.

5 Drain the spaghetti, using a slotted spoon, and transfer to a warm serving dish. Pour the pesto sauce over the spaghetti and then sprinkle over the grated Parmesan cheese.

6 Garnish with oregano sprigs and serve with extra cheese, if using.

VARIATION

For a vegetarian alternative of this recipe, simply substitute drained sun-dried tomatoes for the anchovy fillets.

COOK'S TIP

If you find canned anchovies much too salty, soak them in a saucer of cold milk for 5 minutes, drain, and pat dry with paper towels before using them.

Fettuccine with Anchovy & Spinach Sauce

This colorful starter can be made with a variety of different pasta, including spaghetti and linguine.

Serves 4

INGREDIENTS

2 pounds fresh, young
  spinach leaves
14 ounces dried fettuccine

6 tbsp olive oil
3 tbsp pine nuts
3 garlic cloves, crushed

8 canned anchovy fillets, drained
  and chopped
salt

1 Trim off any tough spinach stalks. Rinse the spinach leaves and place them in a large saucepan with only the water that is clinging to them after washing. Cover and cook over a high heat, shaking the pan from time, until the spinach has wilted, but retains its color. Drain well, set aside and keep warm.

2 Bring a large saucepan of lightly salted water to a boil. Add the fettuccine and 1 tbsp of the oil and cook until it is just tender, but still firm to the bite.

3 Heat 4 tbsp of the remaining olive oil in a saucepan. Add the pine nuts and fry until golden. Remove from the pan and set aside.

4 Add the garlic to the pan and fry until golden. Add the anchovies and stir in the spinach. Cook, stirring, for 2-3 minutes, until heated through. Return the pine nuts to the pan.

5 Drain the fettuccine, toss in the remaining olive oil, and transfer to a warm serving dish.

Spoon the anchovy and spinach sauce over the fettuccine, toss lightly, and serve immediately.

COOK'S TIP

If you are in a hurry, you can use frozen spinach. Thaw and drain it thoroughly, pressing out as much moisture as possible. Cut the leaves into strips and add to the dish with the anchovies in step 4.

Penne with Muscoli Fritti nell' Olio

This is quick and simple, but one of the nicest
of Italian fried fish dishes, served with penne.

Serves 4-6

INGREDIENTS

3^1/$_2$ cups dried penne
^{1}/$_2$ cup olive oil
1 pound mussels, cooked
    and shelled

1 tsp sea salt
^{2}/$_3$ cup all-purpose flour
3^1/$_2$ ounces sun-dried
    tomatoes, sliced

2 tbsp chopped fresh basil leaves
salt and pepper
1 lemon, thinly sliced, to garnish

1 Bring a large saucepan of lightly salted water to a boil. Add the penne and 1 tbsp of the olive oil and cook until the pasta is just tender, but still firm to the bite.

2 Drain the pasta well and place in a large, warm serving dish. Set aside and keep warm while you cook the mussels.

3 Lightly sprinkle the mussels with the sea salt. Season the flour with salt and pepper to taste, sprinkle into a bowl, and toss the mussels in the flour until coated.

4 Heat the remaining oil in a large skillet. Add the mussels and fry, stirring frequently, until golden brown.

5 Toss the mussels with the penne and sprinkle with the sun-dried tomatoes and basil leaves. Garnish with slices of lemon and serve immediately.

VARIATION

You could substitute clams for the mussels. If using fresh clams, try smaller varieties, such as Venus.

COOK'S TIP

Sun-dried tomatoes have been used in Mediterranean countries for a long time, but have become popular elsewhere only quite recently. They are dried and then preserved in oil. They have a concentrated, almost roasted flavor and a dense texture. They should be drained and chopped or sliced before using.

Meat & Poultry

Pasta and meat or poultry is a classic combination. Dishes range from easy, economic mid-week suppers to sophisticated and elegant meals for special occasions. The recipes in this chapter include many family favorites, such as Spaghetti Bolognese, Fresh Spaghetti with Italian Meatballs in Tomato Sauce, Lasagne Verde, and Stuffed Cannelloni. There are also some exciting variations on traditional themes, such as Sicilian Spaghetti, Beef & Pasta Bake, and Stir-fried Pork with Pasta & Vegetables. Finally, there is a superb collection of mouthwatering original recipes. Why not try Fettuccine with Fillet of Veal & Pink Grapefruit in a Rose Petal Butter Sauce, Orecchioni with Pork in Cream Sauce, garnished with Quail Eggs, Chicken & Lobster on a Bed of Penne, or Rigatoni & Pesto Baked Partridge? You will be astonished at how quickly and easily you can prepare these gourmet dishes.

Spaghetti Bolognese

*You can use this classic meat sauce for lasagne, cannelloni,
or any other baked pasta dishes.*

Serves 4

INGREDIENTS

3 tbsp olive oil
2 garlic cloves, crushed
1 large onion, finely chopped
1 carrot, diced
2 cups lean ground beef, veal,
  or chicken

3 ounces chicken livers,
  finely chopped
3¹/₂ ounces lean prosciutto, diced
⁵/₈ cup Marsala
10 ounce can chopped
  plum tomatoes

1 tbsp chopped fresh basil leaves
2 tbsp tomato paste
salt and pepper
1 pound dried spaghetti

1 Heat 2 tbsp of the olive oil in a large saucepan. Add the garlic, onion, and carrot and sauté for 6 minutes.

2 Add the ground beef, veal, or chicken, the chicken livers, and prosciutto to the pan and cook over a medium heat, stirring occasionally, for 12 minutes, until well browned.

3 Stir in the Marsala, tomatoes, basil, and tomato paste and cook for 4 minutes. Season to taste

with salt and pepper. Cover and simmer for about 30 minutes.

4 Remove the lid from the pan, stir, and simmer for a further 15 minutes.

5 Meanwhile, bring a large pan of lightly salted water to a boil. Add the spaghetti and the remaining oil and cook for about 12 minutes, until tender, but still firm to the bite. Drain and transfer to a serving dish. Pour the sauce over the pasta, toss, and serve hot.

VARIATION

Chicken livers are an essential ingredient in a classic Bolognese sauce to which they add richness. However, if you prefer not to use them, you can substitute the same quantity of ground beef.

Creamed Strips of Sirloin with Rigatoni

*This quick and easy dish tastes superb and would
make a delicious treat for a special occasion.*

Serves 4

INGREDIENTS

6 tbsp butter
1 pound sirloin steak, trimmed and
    cut into thin strips
6 ounces button mushrooms, sliced
1 tsp mustard
pinch of freshly grated ginger root

2 tbsp dry sherry
$5/8$ cup heavy cream
salt and pepper
4 slices hot toast, cut into triangles,
    to serve

PASTA:
1 pound dried rigatoni
2 tbsp olive oil
2 fresh basil sprigs
8 tbsp butter

1 Preheat the oven to 375°F. Melt the butter in a large skillet and gently fry the steak over a low heat, stirring frequently, for 6 minutes. Using a slotted spoon, transfer the steak to an ovenproof dish and keep warm.

2 Add the sliced mushrooms to the skillet and cook for 2–3 minutes in the juices remaining in the pan. Add the mustard, ginger, and salt and pepper to taste. Cook for about 2 minutes, then add the sherry

and cream. Cook for a further 3 minutes, then pour the cream sauce over the steak.

3 Bake the steak and cream mixture in the preheated oven for 10 minutes.

4 Meanwhile, cook the pasta. Bring a large saucepan of lightly salted water to a boil. Add the rigatoni, olive oil, and 1 of the basil sprigs and boil rapidly for 10 minutes, until tender but still firm to the bite. Drain the pasta

and transfer to a warm serving plate. Toss the pasta with the butter and garnish with the remaining basil sprig.

5 Serve the steak with the pasta and triangles of warm toast.

COOK'S TIP

Dried pasta will keep for up to 6 months. Keep it in the packet and reseal it once you have opened it, or transfer the pasta to an airtight jar.

Fresh Spaghetti with Italian Meatballs in Tomato Sauce

This well-loved Italian dish is famous across the world. Make the most of it by using high-quality steak for the meatballs.

Serves 4

INGREDIENTS

2¹/₂ cups brown breadcrumbs
⁵/₈ cup milk
2 tbsp butter
¹/₄ cup whole-wheat flour
⁷/₈ cup beef stock
14 ounce can chopped tomatoes

2 tbsp tomato paste
1 tsp sugar
1 tbsp finely chopped fresh tarragon
1 large onion, chopped
4 cups ground steak
1 tsp paprika

4 tbsp olive oil
1 pound fresh spaghetti
salt and pepper
fresh tarragon sprigs, to garnish

1 Place the breadcrumbs in a bowl, add the milk, and set aside to soak for 30 minutes.

2 Melt half the butter in a pan. Add the flour and cook, stirring constantly, for 2 minutes. Gradually stir in the beef stock and cook, stirring constantly, for a further 5 minutes. Add the tomatoes, tomato paste, sugar, and tarragon. Season well and simmer for 25 minutes.

3 Mix the onion, steak, and paprika into the breadcrumbs and season to taste. Shape the mixture into 14 meatballs.

4 Heat the oil and remaining butter in a skillet and fry the meatballs, turning frequently, until brown all over. Place them in a deep casserole, pour the tomato sauce over the meatballs, cover, and bake in a preheated oven at 350°F for 25 minutes.

5 Bring a large saucepan of lightly salted water to a boil. Add the fresh spaghetti, bring back to a boil, and cook for about 2–3 minutes, until tender, but still firm to the bite.

6 Meanwhile, remove the meatballs from the oven and allow them to cool for 3 minutes. Serve the meatballs and their sauce with the spaghetti, garnished with tarragon sprigs.

Layered Meat Loaf

*The cheese-flavored pasta layer comes as a pleasant
surprise inside this lightly spiced meat loaf.*

Serves 6

INGREDIENTS

2 tbsp butter, plus extra
  for greasing
1 small onion, finely chopped
1 small red bell pepper, cored, seeded,
  and chopped
1 garlic clove, chopped
4 cups ground beef
$^{1}/_{2}$ cup white breadcrumbs

$^{1}/_{2}$ tsp cayenne pepper
1 tbsp lemon juice
$^{1}/_{2}$ tsp grated lemon rind
2 tbsp chopped fresh parsley
$^{3}/_{4}$ cup dried short pasta, such
  as fusilli
1 tbsp olive oil
4 bay leaves

1 cup Italian cheese sauce (see
  page 38)
6 ounces bacon
salt and pepper
salad greens, to garnish

---

1 Preheat the oven to 350°F.
Melt the butter in a pan over
a medium heat and sauté the
onion and bell pepper for about
3 minutes. Stir in the garlic and
cook for 1 minute.

2 Put the meat into a bowl and
mash with a wooden spoon
until sticky. Add the onion
mixture, breadcrumbs, cayenne
pepper, lemon juice, lemon rind,
and parsley. Season and set aside.

3 Bring a pan of salted water to
a boil. Add the pasta and oil
and cook for 8–10 minutes, until
almost tender. Drain and stir into
the Italian cheese sauce.

4 Grease a 2-pound loaf pan
and arrange the bay leaves in
the base. Stretch the bacon slices
with the back of a knife and line
the base and sides of the pan with
them. Spoon in half the meat
mixture and smooth the surface.

Cover with the pasta mixed with
Italian cheese sauce, then spoon in
the remaining meat mixture. Level
the top and cover with foil.

5 Bake the meat loaf for 1 hour,
or until the juices run clear
when a skewer is inserted in the
center and the loaf has shrunk
away from the sides. Pour off any
excess fat and turn out the loaf
onto a warm serving dish. Garnish
with salad greens.

Egg Noodles with Beef

*Quick and easy, this mouthwatering Chinese-style
noodle dish can be cooked in minutes.*

Serves 4

INGREDIENTS

10 ounces egg noodles
3 tbsp walnut oil
1-inch piece fresh ginger root, cut
   into thin strips
5 scallions, finely shredded
2 garlic cloves, finely chopped

1 red bell pepper, cored, seeded, and
   thinly sliced
3 1/2 ounces button mushrooms,
   thinly sliced
12 ounces fillet steak, cut into
   thin strips
1 tbsp cornstarch

5 tbsp dry sherry
3 tbsp soy sauce
1 tsp soft brown sugar
1 cup bean sprouts
1 tbsp sesame oil
salt and pepper
scallion strips, to garnish

1 Bring a large saucepan of
water to a boil. Add the
noodles and cook according to the
instructions on the packet. Drain
the noodles thoroughly, set aside
and keep warm.

2 Heat the walnut oil in a
preheated wok. Add the
ginger, scallions, and garlic and
stir-fry for 45 seconds. Add the
bell pepper, mushrooms, and steak
and stir-fry for 4 minutes. Season
to taste with salt and pepper.

3 Mix together the cornstarch,
sherry, and soy sauce in a
small bowl to form a paste, and
pour into the wok. Sprinkle in
the brown sugar and stir-fry all
of the ingredients for a further
2 minutes.

4 Add the bean sprouts, drained
noodles, and sesame oil to the
wok, stir and toss together for
1 minute. Transfer to serving
plates, garnish with strips of
scallion and serve immediately.

COOK'S TIP

*If you do not have a wok, you could
prepare this dish in a skillet.
However, a wok is preferable, as
the round base ensures an even
distribution of heat and it is easier
to keep stirring and tossing the
contents when stir-frying.*

Tagliarini with Meatballs in Red Wine & Oyster Mushroom Sauce

A different twist is given to this traditional pasta dish with a rich, but subtle, sauce.

Serves 4

INGREDIENTS

2 cups white breadcrumbs
$5/8$ cup milk
2 tbsp butter
9 tbsp olive oil
3 cups sliced
   oyster mushrooms
$1/4$ cup whole-wheat flour
$7/8$ cup beef stock

$5/8$ cup red wine
4 tomatoes, skinned and chopped
1 tbsp tomato paste
1 tsp brown sugar
1 tbsp finely chopped fresh basil
12 shallots, chopped
4 cups ground steak
1 tsp paprika

1 pound dried egg tagliarini
salt and pepper
fresh basil sprigs, to garnish

1 Soak the breadcrumbs in the milk for 30 minutes.

2 Heat half the butter and 4 tbsp of the oil in a pan. Sauté the mushrooms for 4 minutes, then stir in the flour and cook for 2 minutes. Add the stock and wine and simmer for 15 minutes. Add the tomatoes, tomato paste, sugar, and basil. Season well and simmer for 30 minutes.

3 Mix the shallots, steak, and paprika with the breadcrumbs and season. Shape the mixture into 14 meatballs.

4 Heat 4 tbsp of the remaining oil and the remaining butter in a large skillet. Fry the meatballs, turning frequently, until brown all over. Transfer to a deep casserole, pour in the red wine and the mushroom sauce, cover, and bake

in a preheated oven at 350°F for 30 minutes.

5 Bring a pan of salted water to a boil. Add the pasta and the remaining oil and cook until tender. Drain and transfer to a serving dish. Remove the casserole from the oven and cool for 3 minutes. Pour the meatballs and sauce onto the pasta, garnish with the basil sprigs, and serve.

Sicilian Spaghetti

This delicious Sicilian dish originated as a handy way of using up leftover cooked pasta.

Serves 4

INGREDIENTS

⁵/₈ cup olive oil, plus extra for
   brushing
2 eggplants
3 cups ground beef
1 onion, chopped
2 garlic cloves, crushed
2 tbsp tomato paste
14 ounce can chopped tomatoes
1 tsp Worcestershire sauce

1 tsp chopped fresh marjoram or
   oregano or ¹/₂ tsp dried marjoram
   or oregano
¹/₂ cup pitted black olives, sliced
1 green, red, or yellow bell pepper,
   cored, seeded, and chopped
6 ounces dried spaghetti
1 cup freshly grated Parmesan
   cheese

salt and pepper
fresh oregano or parsley sprigs,
   to garnish

1 Brush an 8-inch loose-based round cake pan with oil, line the base with baking parchment, and brush with oil.

2 Slice the eggplant. Heat a little olive oil in a pan and fry the eggplant, in batches if necessary, until browned on both sides. Add more oil as necessary. Drain on paper towels.

3 Put the beef, onion, and garlic in a saucepan and cook over a medium heat, stirring until browned. Add the tomato paste, tomatoes, Worcestershire sauce, marjoram or oregano, and salt and pepper. Simmer, stirring occasionally, for 10 minutes. Add the olives and bell pepper and cook for a further 10 minutes.

4 Bring a pan of salted water to a boil. Add the spaghetti and 1 tablespoon of olive oil and cook until tender, but still firm to the bite. Drain and turn the spaghetti into a bowl. Add the meat mixture and cheese and toss together with 2 forks.

5 Arrange eggplant slices over the base and up the sides of the cake pan. Add the spaghetti and then cover with the rest of the eggplant slices. Bake in a preheated oven at 400°F for 40 minutes. Let stand for 5 minutes, then invert onto a serving dish. Discard the baking parchment. Garnish with the fresh herbs and serve.

Beef & Pasta Bake

The combination of macaroni and beef korma gives this a really authentic flavor.

Serves 4

INGREDIENTS

2 pounds steak, cut into cubes
about ½ cup beef stock
1 pound dried macaroni
1¼ cups heavy cream
½ tsp garam masala
salt
fresh cilantro, to garnish
naan bread, to serve

KORMA PASTE:
½ cup blanched almonds
6 garlic cloves
1-inch piece fresh ginger root,
  coarsely chopped
6 tbsp beef stock
1 tsp ground cardamom
4 cloves, crushed

1 tsp cinnamon
2 large onions, chopped
1 tsp coriander seeds
2 tsp ground cumin seeds
pinch of cayenne pepper
6 tbsp of sunflower oil

1 To make the korma paste, grind the almonds finely using a pestle and mortar. Put the ground almonds and the rest of the korma paste ingredients into a food processor or blender and process well to make a very smooth paste.

2 Put the steak in a shallow dish and spoon over the korma paste, turning to coat the steak well. Leave in the refrigerator to marinate for 6 hours.

3 Transfer the steak with the marinade to a large saucepan, and simmer over a low heat, adding a little beef stock if required, for 35 minutes.

4 Meanwhile, bring a large saucepan of lightly salted water to a boil. Add the macaroni and cook for 10 minutes, until tender, but still firm to the bite. Drain the pasta and transfer to a deep casserole. Add the steak, heavy cream, and garam masala.

5 Bake in a preheated oven at 400°F for 30 minutes. Remove the casserole from the oven and allow to stand for about 10 minutes. Garnish with fresh cilantro and serve with naan bread.

VARIATION

You could also make this dish using diced chicken and chicken stock, instead of steak and beef stock.

Lasagne Verde

Today you can buy precooked lasagne sheets from most supermarkets; otherwise prepare the lasagne sheets according to the instructions on the packet.

Serves 4–6

INGREDIENTS

butter, for greasing
14 sheets precooked lasagne
3³/₄ cups béchamel sauce (see page 166)
³/₄ cup grated mozzarella cheese
fresh basil (optional), to garnish

MEAT SAUCE:
¹/₈ cup olive oil
4 cups ground beef
1 large onion, chopped
1 celery stalk, diced
4 cloves garlic, crushed
¹/₄ cup all-purpose flour
1¹/₄ cups beef stock
⁵/₈ cup red wine

1 tbsp chopped fresh parsley
1 tsp chopped fresh marjoram
1 tsp chopped fresh basil
2 tbsp tomato paste
salt and pepper

1 To make the meat sauce, heat the olive oil in a large skillet. Add the ground beef and cook, stirring frequently, until browned all over. Add the onion, celery, and garlic and cook for 3 minutes.

2 Sprinkle in the flour and cook, stirring constantly, for 1 minute. Gradually stir in the stock and red wine, season well with salt and pepper, and add the parsley, marjoram, and basil. Bring to a boil, lower the heat, and simmer for 35 minutes. Add the tomato paste and simmer for a further 10 minutes.

3 Lightly grease an ovenproof dish with a little butter. Arrange sheets of lasagne over the base of the dish, spoon a layer of meat sauce over the noodles, then béchamel sauce. Place another layer of lasagne on top and repeat the whole process twice, finishing with a layer of béchamel sauce. Lightly sprinkle with the grated mozzarella cheese.

4 Bake the lasagne in a preheated oven at 375°F for 35 minutes, until the top is golden brown and bubbling. Garnish with fresh basil, if desired, and serve immediately.

Pasticcio

A recipe with both Italian and Greek origins, this dish
may be served hot or cold, cut into thick, satisfying squares.

Serves 6

INGREDIENTS

2 cups dried fusilli
1 tbsp olive oil, plus extra
   for brushing
4 tbsp heavy cream
salt
fresh rosemary sprigs, to garnish
mixed salad, to serve

SAUCE:
2 tbsp olive oil
1 onion, thinly sliced

1 red bell pepper, cored, seeded,
   and chopped
2 garlic cloves, chopped
5$^{1}/_{4}$ cups ground beef
14 ounce can chopped tomatoes
$^{1}/_{2}$ cup dry white wine
2 tbsp chopped fresh parsley
2 ounce can anchovies, drained
   and chopped
salt and pepper

TOPPING:
1$^{1}/_{4}$ cups natural yogurt
3 eggs
pinch of freshly grated nutmeg
$^{1}/_{2}$ cup freshly grated Parmesan
   cheese

1 To make the sauce, heat the oil in a skillet and sauté the onion and red bell pepper for 3 minutes. Add the garlic and cook for 1 minute. Add the beef and cook until browned.

2 Add the tomatoes and wine to the skillet and bring to a boil. Lower the heat and simmer for 20 minutes, until thickened.

Stir in the parsley and anchovies and season to taste.

3 Bring a pan of salted water to a boil. Add the pasta and oil and cook for 10 minutes, until almost tender. Drain and transfer to a bowl. Stir in the cream.

4 For the topping, beat the yogurt, eggs, and nutmeg.

5 Brush an ovenproof dish with oil. Spoon in half the pasta and cover with half the meat sauce. Repeat the process, then spread on the topping and sprinkle with cheese.

6 Bake in a preheated oven at 375°F for 25 minutes until golden. Garnish with rosemary and serve with a mixed salad.

Fettuccine with Fillet of Veal & Pink Grapefruit in a Rose Petal Butter Sauce

This truly spectacular dish is equally delicious whether you use veal or pork fillet.
Make sure the roses are free of blemishes and pesticides.

Serves 4

INGREDIENTS

1 pound dried fettuccine
7 tbsp olive oil
1 tsp chopped fresh oregano
1 tsp chopped fresh marjoram
$^3/_4$ cup butter
1 pound veal fillet, thinly sliced

$^5/_8$ cup rose petal vinegar (see
  Cook's Tip)
$^5/_8$ cup fish stock
$^1/_4$ cup grapefruit juice
$^1/_4$ cup heavy cream
salt

TO GARNISH:
12 pink grapefruit segments
12 pink peppercorns
rose petals
fresh herb leaves

1 Bring a pan of lightly salted water to a boil. Add the fettuccine and 1 tbsp of the oil and cook for 12 minutes, until tender, but still firm to the bite. Drain and transfer to a warm serving dish. Add 2 tbsp of the olive oil, the oregano, and marjoram.

2 Heat 4 tbsp of the butter with the remaining oil in a large skillet. Add the veal and cook over a low heat for 6 minutes. Remove from the skillet and place on top of the pasta.

3 Add the vinegar and fish stock to the pan and bring to a boil. Boil vigorously until reduced by two-thirds. Add the grapefruit juice and cream and simmer over a low heat for 4 minutes. Dice the remaining butter and add to the pan, one piece at a time, whisking constantly until it has been completely incorporated.

4 Pour the sauce around the veal, garnish with grapefruit segments, pink peppercorns, the rose petals (washed), and your favorite herb leaves.

COOK'S TIP

To make rose petal vinegar, infuse the petals of 8 pesticide-free roses in $^5/_8$ cup white wine vinegar for 48 hours.

Neapolitan Veal Cutlets with Mascarpone Cheese & Marille

The delicious combination of apple, onion, and mushroom
perfectly complements the delicate flavor of veal.

Serves 4

INGREDIENTS

$^7/_8$ cup butter

4 x 9 ounce veal cutlets, trimmed

1 large onion, sliced

2 apples, peeled, cored, and sliced

6 ounces button mushrooms

1 tbsp chopped fresh tarragon

8 black peppercorns

1 tbsp sesame seeds

14 ounces dried marille

$^1/_2$ cup extra virgin olive oil

$^3/_4$ cup mascarpone cheese, broken
 into small pieces

salt and pepper

2 large beef tomatoes, cut in half

leaves of 1 fresh basil sprig

fresh basil leaves, to garnish

1 Melt 4 tbsp of the butter in a skillet. Fry the veal over a low heat for 5 minutes on each side. Transfer to a dish and keep warm.

2 Fry the onion and apples in the pan until lightly browned. Transfer to a dish, place the veal on top, and keep warm.

3 Melt the remaining butter in the skillet. Gently cook the mushrooms, tarragon, and peppercorns over a low heat for 3 minutes. Sprinkle with the sesame seeds.

4 Bring a pan of salted water to a boil. Add the pasta and 1 tbsp of the oil. Cook until tender, but still firm to the bite. Drain thoroughly and transfer to a serving plate.

5 Top the pasta with the mascarpone cheese and sprinkle with the remaining olive oil. Place the onions, apples and veal cutlets on top of the pasta. Spoon the mushrooms, peppercorns, and pan juices onto the cutlets, place the tomatoes and basil leaves around the edge, and place in a preheated oven at 300°F for 5 minutes.

6 Season to taste with salt and pepper, garnish with fresh basil leaves, and serve immediately.

Stir-fried Pork with Pasta & Vegetables

*This delicious dish, with its hint of Thai cuisine,
will certainly get the taste buds tingling.*

Serves 4

INGREDIENTS

3 tbsp sesame oil
12 ounces pork tenderloin, cut into
   thin strips
1 pound dried taglioni
1 tbsp olive oil
8 shallots, sliced
2 garlic cloves, finely chopped

1-inch piece fresh ginger
   root, grated
1 fresh green chili, finely chopped
1 red bell pepper, cored, seeded,
   and thinly sliced
1 green bell pepper, cored, seeded,
   and thinly sliced

3 zucchini, thinly sliced
2 tbsp ground almonds
1 tsp ground cinnamon
1 tbsp oyster sauce
2 ounces creamed coconut (see
   Cook's Tip), grated
salt and pepper

1 Heat the sesame oil in a preheated wok. Season the pork with salt and black pepper, add to the wok, and stir-fry for 5 minutes.

2 Meanwhile, bring a large saucepan of lightly salted water to a boil. Add the taglioni and olive oil and cook for about 12 minutes, until just tender, but still firm to the bite. Set the pasta aside and keep warm until it is required.

3 Add the shallots, garlic, ginger, and chili to the wok and stir-fry for 2 minutes. Add the bell peppers and zucchini and stir-fry for 1 minute.

4 Finally, add the ground almonds, cinnamon, oyster sauce, and creamed coconut to the wok and stir-fry for 1 minute.

5 Drain the taglioni and transfer to a serving dish. Top with the stir-fry and serve immediately.

COOK'S TIP

Creamed coconut is available from Chinese and Asian food stores and some large supermarkets. It is sold in the form of compressed blocks and adds a concentrated coconut flavor to the dish.

Orecchioni with Pork in Cream Sauce, garnished with Quail Eggs

This unusual and attractive dish is surprisingly quick and easy to make.

Serves 4

INGREDIENTS

1 pound pork tenderloin,
  thinly sliced
4 tbsp olive oil
8 ounces button mushrooms, sliced

$^7/_8$ cup Italian red wine sauce (see
  page 52)
1 tbsp lemon juice
pinch of saffron

3 cups dried orecchioni
4 tbsp heavy cream
12 quail eggs (see Cook's Tip)
salt

1 Pound the slices of pork between 2 sheets of plastic wrap until they are wafer thin, then cut into strips.

2 Heat the olive oil in a large skillet, add the pork, and stir-fry for 5 minutes. Add the mushrooms to the pan and stir-fry for a further 2 minutes.

3 Pour in the Italian red wine sauce, lower the heat, and leave the mixture to simmer gently for 20 minutes.

4 Meanwhile, bring a large saucepan of lightly salted water to a boil. Add the lemon juice, saffron, and orecchioni and cook for 12 minutes, until tender but still firm to the bite. Drain the pasta and keep warm.

5 Stir the cream into the pan with the pork and heat gently for a few minutes.

6 Boil the quail eggs for 3 minutes, cool them in cold water, and remove the shells.

7 Transfer the pasta to a large, warm serving plate, top with the pork and sauce, and garnish with the eggs. Serve immediately.

COOK'S TIP

In this recipe, the quail eggs are soft-cooked. As they are extremely difficult to shell when warm, it is important that they are thoroughly cooled first. Otherwise, they will break up unattractively.

Stuffed Cannelloni

Cannelloni, the thick, round pasta tubes, make perfect containers for close-textured sauces of all kinds.

Serves 4

INGREDIENTS

8 dried cannelloni tubes
1 tbsp olive oil
$\frac{1}{4}$ cup freshly grated Parmesan
  cheese
fresh herb sprigs, to garnish

FILLING:
2 tbsp butter

10$\frac{1}{2}$ ounces frozen spinach, thawed
  and chopped
$\frac{1}{2}$ cup ricotta cheese
$\frac{1}{4}$ cup freshly grated
  Parmesan cheese
$\frac{1}{4}$ cup chopped ham
pinch of freshly grated nutmeg
2 tbsp heavy cream
2 eggs, lightly beaten

salt and pepper

SAUCE:
2 tbsp butter
$\frac{1}{4}$ cup all-purpose flour
1$\frac{1}{4}$ cups milk
2 bay leaves
pinch of freshly grated nutmeg

1 To make the filling, melt the butter in a pan and stir-fry the spinach for 2–3 minutes. Remove from the heat and stir in the ricotta and Parmesan cheeses and the ham. Season with nutmeg, salt, and pepper. Beat in the cream and eggs to make a thick paste.

2 Bring a pan of lightly salted water to a boil. Add the pasta and the oil and cook for 10–12 minutes, until almost tender. Drain and set aside to cool.

3 To make the sauce, melt the butter in a pan. Stir in the flour and cook, stirring, for 1 minute. Gradually stir in the milk. Add the bay leaves and simmer, stirring, for 5 minutes. Add the nutmeg, salt, and pepper. Remove from the heat and discard the bay leaves.

4 Spoon the filling into a piping bag and fill the cannelloni.

5 Spoon a little sauce into the base of an ovenproof dish. Arrange the cannelloni in the dish in a single layer and pour over the remaining sauce. Sprinkle with the Parmesan cheese and bake in a preheated oven at 375°F for 40–45 minutes. Garnish with fresh herb sprigs and serve.

Tagliatelle with Pumpkin

This unusual dish comes from the Emilia Romagna region.
Why not serve it with Lambrusco, the local wine?

Serves 4

INGREDIENTS

1 pound 2 ounces pumpkin or
  butternut squash, peeled
  and seeded
3 tbsp olive oil
1 onion, finely chopped
2 garlic cloves, crushed

4–6 tbsp chopped fresh parsley
pinch of freshly grated nutmeg
about 1¼ cups chicken or
  vegetable stock
4 ounces prosciutto
9 ounces dried tagliatelle

⅝ cup heavy cream
salt and pepper
freshly grated Parmesan cheese,
  to serve

1 Cut the pumpkin or
butternut squash in half and
scoop out the seeds with a spoon.
Cut the pumpkin or squash into
½-inch cubes.

2 Heat 2 tbsp of the olive oil in
a large saucepan. Add the
onion and garlic and fry over a
low heat for about 3 minutes,
until soft. Add half of the parsley
and cook for 1 minute.

3 Add the pumpkin or squash
pieces and cook for

2–3 minutes. Season to taste with
salt, pepper, and nutmeg.

4 Add half of the stock to the
pan, bring to a boil, cover,
and leave to simmer for about
10 minutes, or until the pumpkin
or squash is tender. Add more
stock if the pumpkin or squash is
becoming dry and looks as if it
might burn.

5 Add the prosciutto to the pan
and cook, stirring frequently,
for a further 2 minutes.

6 Meanwhile, bring a large
saucepan of lightly salted
water to a boil. Add the tagliatelle
and the remaining oil and cook for
12 minutes, until tender, but
still firm to the bite. Drain the
pasta and transfer to a warm
serving dish.

7 Stir the cream into the
pumpkin and ham mixture
and heat through. Spoon over the
pasta, sprinkle with the remaining
parsley, and serve. Serve the grated
Parmesan separately.

Eggplant Cake

Layers of toasty-brown eggplant, meat sauce, and cheese-flavored pasta make this a popular family supper dish.

Serves 4

INGREDIENTS

1 eggplant, thinly sliced
5 tbsp olive oil
2 cups dried fusilli
2½ cups béchamel sauce (see page 166)
¾ cup grated cheddar cheese
butter, for greasing

⅓ cup freshly grated Parmesan cheese
salt and pepper

LAMB SAUCE:
2 tbsp olive oil
1 large onion, sliced
2 celery stalks, thinly sliced

1 pound ground lamb
3 tbsp tomato paste
5½ ounces bottled sun-dried tomatoes, drained and chopped
1 tsp dried oregano
1 tbsp red wine vinegar
⅝ cup chicken stock
salt and pepper

1 Put the eggplant slices in a colander, sprinkle with salt, and set aside for 45 minutes to remove the bitter juices.

2 To make the lamb sauce, heat the oil in a pan. Add the onion and celery and sauté for 3–4 minutes. Add the lamb and cook, stirring frequently, until browned. Stir in the remaining sauce ingredients, bring to a boil, and cook for 20 minutes.

3 Rinse the eggplant slices, drain, and pat dry. Heat 4 tbsp of the oil in a skillet. Fry the eggplant slices for about 4 minutes on each side. Remove from the skillet and drain well.

4 Bring a large pan of lightly salted water to a boil. Add the fusilli and the remaining oil and cook until almost tender, but still firm to the bite. Drain thoroughly, keep warm and set aside.

5 Gently heat the béchamel sauce, stirring constantly. Stir in the cheddar cheese until well combined. Stir half of the cheese sauce into the fusilli.

6 Make layers of fusilli, lamb sauce, and eggplant slices in a greased dish. Spread the remaining cheese sauce over the top. Sprinkle with the Parmesan cheese and bake in a preheated oven at 375°F for 25 minutes. Serve hot or cold.

Whole-wheat Spaghetti with Suprêmes of Chicken Nell Gwyn

The refreshing combination of chicken and orange sauce
makes this a perfect dish for a warm summer evening.

Serves 4

INGREDIENTS

$^{1}/_{8}$ cup rapeseed oil

3 tbsp olive oil

4 x 8 ounce chicken suprêmes

$^{5}/_{8}$ cup orange brandy

2 tbsp all-purpose flour

$^{5}/_{8}$ cup freshly squeezed orange juice

1 ounce zucchini, cut into
matchstick strips

1 ounce red bell pepper, cut into
matchstick strips

1 ounce leek, finely shredded

14 ounces dried whole-
wheat spaghetti

3 large oranges, peeled and cut
into segments

rind of 1 orange, cut into very
fine strips

2 tbsp chopped fresh tarragon

$^{5}/_{8}$ cup fromage frais or
ricotta cheese

salt and pepper

fresh tarragon leaves, to garnish

1 Heat the rapeseed oil and 1 tbsp of the olive oil in a skillet. Add the chicken and cook quickly until golden brown. Add the orange brandy and cook for 3 minutes. Add the flour and cook for 2 minutes.

2 Lower the heat and add the orange juice, zucchini, bell pepper, and leek, and season. Simmer for 5 minutes until the sauce has thickened.

3 Meanwhile, bring a pan of salted water to a boil. Add the spaghetti and 1 tbsp of the olive oil and cook for 10 minutes. Drain, transfer to a serving dish, and drizzle the remaining oil on top.

4 Add half the orange segments, half the orange rind, the tarragon, and fromage frais or ricotta cheese to the sauce in the pan and cook for 3 minutes.

5 Place the chicken on top of the pasta, pour over a little sauce, garnish with orange segments, rind, and tarragon, and serve.

Chicken & Mushroom Lasagne

*You can use your favorite mushrooms, such as chanterelles or
oyster mushrooms, for this delicately flavored dish.*

Serves 4

INGREDIENTS

butter, for greasing
14 sheets precooked lasagne
3³/4 cups béchamel sauce (see page 166)
1 cup grated Parmesan cheese

CHICKEN & MUSHROOM SAUCE:
2 tbsp olive oil
2 garlic cloves, crushed
1 large onion, finely chopped
8 ounces exotic mushrooms, sliced
2¹/2 cups ground chicken
3 ounces chicken livers, finely chopped

4 ounces prosciutto, diced
⁵/8 cup Marsala
10 ounce can chopped tomatoes
1 tbsp chopped fresh basil leaves
2 tbsp tomato paste
salt and pepper

1 To make the chicken and mushroom sauce, heat the olive oil in a large saucepan. Add the garlic, onion, and mushrooms and cook, stirring frequently, for 6 minutes.

2 Add the ground chicken, chicken livers, and prosciutto and cook over a low heat for 12 minutes, until the meat has browned.

3 Stir the Marsala, tomatoes, basil, and tomato paste into the mixture in the pan and cook for 4 minutes. Season to taste with salt and pepper, cover, and simmer for 30 minutes. Uncover the pan, stir, and simmer for a further 15 minutes.

4 Lightly grease an ovenproof dish with butter. Arrange sheets of lasagne over the base of the dish, spoon a layer of chicken and mushroom sauce over the lasagne, then add a layer of béchamel sauce. Place another layer of lasagne on top and repeat the process twice, finishing with a layer of béchamel sauce. Lightly sprinkle with the grated cheese and bake in a preheated oven at 375°F for 35 minutes until a golden brown color and bubbling. Serve immediately.

Tagliatelle with Chicken Sauce

Spinach ribbon noodles with a rich tomato sauce and topped with creamy chicken make a very appetizing dish.

Serves 4

INGREDIENTS

9 ounces fresh green tagliatelle
1 tbsp olive oil
salt
fresh basil leaves, to garnish

TOMATO SAUCE:
2 tbsp olive oil
1 small onion, chopped

1 garlic clove, chopped
14 ounce can chopped tomatoes
2 tbsp chopped fresh parsley
1 tsp dried oregano
2 bay leaves
2 tbsp tomato paste
1 tsp sugar
salt and pepper

CHICKEN SAUCE:
4 tbsp unsalted butter
14 ounces boned chicken breasts,
   skinned, and cut into thin strips
$^3/_4$ cup blanched almonds
$1^1/_4$ cups heavy cream
salt and pepper

1 To make the tomato sauce, heat the oil in a pan over a medium heat. Add the onion and sauté until translucent. Add the garlic and cook for 1 minute. Stir in the tomatoes, fresh oregano, bay leaves, tomato paste, sugar, and a little salt and pepper to taste, bring to a boil, and simmer, uncovered, for 15–20 minutes, until reduced by half. Remove the pan from the heat and discard the bay leaves.

2 To make the chicken sauce, melt the butter in a skillet over a medium heat. Add the chicken and almonds and stir-fry for 5–6 minutes, until the chicken is cooked through.

3 Meanwhile, bring the cream to a boil in a small pan over a low heat and boil for about 10 minutes, until reduced by almost half. Pour the cream over the chicken and almonds, stir, and

season to taste with salt and pepper. Set aside and keep warm.

4 Bring a large pan of lightly salted water to a boil. Add the tagliatelle and olive oil and cook until tender, but still firm to the bite. Drain and transfer to a warm serving dish. Spoon the tomato sauce over the pasta and arrange the chicken sauce down the center. Garnish with the basil leaves and serve immediately.

Mustard Baked Chicken with Pasta Shells

Chicken pieces are cooked in a succulent, mild mustard sauce, then coated in poppy seeds, and served on a bed of fresh pasta shells.

Serves 4

INGREDIENTS

8 chicken pieces
   (about 4 ounces each)
4 tbsp butter, melted
4 tbsp mild mustard (see Cook's Tip)

2 tbsp lemon juice
1 tbsp brown sugar
1 tsp paprika
3 tbsp poppy seeds

14 ounces fresh pasta shells
1 tbsp olive oil
salt and pepper

1 Arrange the chicken pieces, smooth side down, in a single layer in a large ovenproof dish.

2 Mix together the butter, mustard, lemon juice, sugar, and paprika in a bowl and season to taste with salt and pepper. Brush the mixture over the upper surfaces of the chicken pieces and bake in a preheated oven at 400°F for 15 minutes.

3 Remove the dish from the oven and carefully turn over the chicken pieces. Coat the upper surfaces of the chicken with the remaining mustard mixture, sprinkle the chicken pieces with poppy seeds, and return to the oven for a further 15 minutes.

4 Meanwhile, bring a large pan of lightly salted water to a boil. Add the pasta shells and olive oil and cook until tender, but still firm to the bite.

5 Drain the pasta and arrange on a warmed serving dish.

Top with the chicken, pour the sauce on, and serve immediately.

COOK'S TIP

Dijon is the type of mustard most often used in cooking, as it has a clean and only mildly spicy flavor. German mustard has a sweet-sour taste, with Bavarian mustard being slightly sweeter. American mustard is mild and sweet.

Tortellini

Tortellini were said to have been created in the image of the goddess Venus's navel. Whatever the story, these delicate filled pasta swirls offer a delicious blend of Italian flavors.

Serves 4

INGREDIENTS

4 ounces boned chicken
  breast, skinned
2 ounces prosciutto
1¹/₂ ounces cooked spinach,
  well drained
1 tbsp finely chopped onion
2 tbsp freshly grated
  Parmesan cheese

pinch of ground allspice
1 egg, beaten
1 pound Basic Pasta Dough (see
  page 4)
salt and pepper
2 tbsp chopped fresh parsley,
  to garnish

SAUCE:
1¹/₄ cups light cream
2 garlic cloves, crushed
4 ounces button mushrooms,
  thinly sliced
4 tbsp freshly grated Parmesan
  cheese

1 Bring a pan of seasoned water to a boil. Add the chicken and poach for about 10 minutes. Cool slightly, then put in a food processor, with the prosciutto, spinach, and onion, and process until finely chopped. Stir in the Parmesan cheese, allspice, and egg and season to taste.

2 Thinly roll out the pasta dough and cut into 1½–2-inch rounds.

3 Place ½ tsp of the filling in the center of each round. Fold the pieces in half and press the edges to seal. Then wrap each piece around your index finger, cross over the ends, and curl the rest of the dough backward to make a navel shape. Re-roll the trimmings and repeat until all the dough is used up.

4 Bring a pan of salted water to a boil. Add the tortellini, in batches, bring back to a boil, and cook for 5 minutes. Drain and transfer to a serving dish.

5 To make the sauce, bring the cream and garlic to a boil in a pan, then simmer for 3 minutes. Add the mushrooms and half the cheese, season, and simmer for 2–3 minutes. Pour the sauce over the tortellini. Sprinkle with the remaining Parmesan cheese, garnish with the parsley and serve.

Chicken Suprêmes Filled with Tiger Shrimp on a Bed of Pasta

These mouthwatering mini-packets of chicken and shrimp will delight your guests.

Serves 4

INGREDIENTS

4 tbsp butter, plus extra
   for greasing
4 x 7 ounce chicken
   suprêmes, trimmed
4 ounces large spinach leaves,
   trimmed and blanched in hot
   salted water

4 slices of prosciutto
12–16 raw tiger shrimp, shelled
   and deveined
1 pound dried tagliatelle
1 tbsp olive oil
3 leeks, shredded
1 large carrot, grated

$5/8$ cup thick mayonnaise
2 large cooked beets
salt

1 Grease 4 large pieces of foil and set aside. Place each suprême between 2 pieces of waxed paper and pound with a rolling pin to flatten.

2 Divide half of the spinach among the suprêmes, add a slice of prosciutto to each, and top with more spinach. Place 3–4 shrimp on top of the spinach. Fold the pointed end of the suprême over the shrimp, then fold over again to form a packet. Wrap in foil, place on a cookie sheet and bake in a preheated oven at 400°F for 20 minutes.

3 Meanwhile, bring a pan of salted water to a boil. Add the tagliatelle and oil and cook until tender. Drain, transfer to a serving dish, set aside and keep warm.

4 Melt the butter in a skillet. Sauté the leeks and carrots for 3 minutes. Transfer the vegetables to the center of the pasta.

5 Work the mayonnaise and 1 beet in a food processor or blender until smooth. Rub through a strainer and pour around the pasta and vegetables.

6 Cut the remaining beet into diamond shapes and place them neatly around the mayonnaise. Remove the foil from the chicken and, using a sharp knife, cut the suprêmes into thin slices. Arrange the slices on top of the vegetables and pasta, and serve.

Chicken & Lobster on a Bed of Penne

While this is certainly a treat to get the taste buds
tingling, it is not as extravagant as it sounds.

Serves 6

INGREDIENTS

butter, for greasing	salt	1 tbsp Marsala
6 chicken breasts		2 tbsp breadcrumbs
1 pound dried penne rigate	FILLING:	1 large egg, beaten
6 tbsp extra virgin olive oil	4 ounces lobster meat, chopped	salt and pepper
1 cup freshly grated	2 shallots, very finely chopped	
Parmesan cheese	2 figs, chopped	

1 Grease 6 pieces of foil large enough to enclose each chicken breast and lightly grease a cookie sheet.

2 Place all of the filling ingredients into a mixing bowl and blend together thoroughly with a spoon.

3 Cut a pocket in each chicken breast with a sharp knife and fill with the lobster mixture. Wrap each chicken breast in foil, place the packets on the greased cookie sheet, and bake in a preheated oven at 400°F for 30 minutes.

4 Meanwhile, bring a large pan of lightly salted water to a boil. Add the pasta and 1 tablespoon of the olive oil and cook for about 10 minutes, or until tender but still firm to the bite. Drain the pasta thoroughly and transfer to a large serving plate. Sprinkle with the remaining olive oil and the grated Parmesan cheese, set aside, and keep warm until required.

5 Carefully remove the foil from around the chicken breasts. Slice the breasts very thinly, arrange over the pasta, and serve immediately.

COOK'S TIP

The cut of chicken known as suprême consists of the breast and wing. It is always skinned.

Chicken with Green Olives & Pasta

*Olives are a popular flavoring for poultry and game in the
Apulia region of Italy, where this recipe originates.*

Serves 4

INGREDIENTS

3 tbsp olive oil
2 tbsp butter
4 chicken breasts, part boned
1 large onion, finely chopped
2 garlic cloves, crushed
2 red, yellow, or green bell peppers,
   cored, seeded, and cut into
   large pieces

9 ounces button mushrooms, sliced
   or quartered
6 ounces tomatoes, skinned
   and halved
5/8 cup dry white wine
1 1/2 cups pitted green olives
4–6 tbsp heavy cream
14 ounces dried pasta

salt and pepper
chopped parsley, to garnish

1 Heat 2 tbsp of the oil and the butter in a skillet. Add the chicken breasts and fry until golden brown. Remove the chicken from the pan.

2 Add the onion and garlic to the pan and sauté over a medium heat until beginning to soften. Add the bell peppers and mushrooms and cook for 2–3 minutes. Add the tomatoes and season to taste with salt and pepper. Transfer the vegetables to a casserole and arrange the chicken on top.

3 Add the wine to the pan and bring to a boil. Pour the wine over the chicken. Cover and cook in a preheated oven at 350°F for 50 minutes.

4 Add the olives to the casserole and mix in until well combined. Pour in the cream, cover, and return to the oven for 10–20 minutes.

5 Meanwhile, bring a large pan of lightly salted water to a boil. Add the pasta and the remaining oil and cook until tender, but still firm to the bite. Drain the pasta well and transfer to a serving dish.

6 Arrange the chicken on top of the pasta, cover with the sauce, garnish with the parsley, and serve immediately. Alternatively, place the pasta in a large serving bowl and serve separately.

Sliced Breast of Duckling with Linguine

A raspberry and honey sauce superbly counterbalances the richness of the duckling.

Serves 4

INGREDIENTS

4 x 10¹/₂ ounce boned breasts
   of duckling
2 tbsp butter
³/₈ cup finely chopped carrots
4 tbsp finely chopped shallots
1 tbsp lemon juice
⁵/₈ cup meat stock
4 tbsp clear honey

³/₄ cup fresh or thawed
   frozen raspberries
¹/₄ cup all-purpose flour
1 tbsp Worcestershire sauce
14 ounces fresh linguine
1 tbsp olive oil
salt and pepper

TO GARNISH:
fresh raspberries
fresh sprigs of parsley

1 Trim and score the duck breasts with a sharp knife and season well all over. Melt the butter in a skillet, add the duck breasts, and fry all over until lightly colored.

2 Add the carrots, shallots, lemon juice, and half the meat stock and simmer over a low heat for 1 minute. Stir in half the honey and half the raspberries. Sprinkle in half the flour and cook, stirring constantly, for

3 minutes. Season with pepper and add the Worcestershire sauce.

3 Stir in the remaining stock and cook for 1 minute. Stir in the remaining honey and remaining raspberries and sprinkle in the remaining flour. Cook for a further 3 minutes.

4 Remove the duck breasts from the pan, but leave the sauce to continue simmering over a very low heat.

5 Meanwhile, bring a large saucepan of lightly salted water to a boil. Add the linguine and olive oil and cook until tender, but still firm to the bite. Drain and divide between 4 individual plates.

6 Slice the duck breasts lengthwise into ¹/₄-inch thick pieces. Pour a little sauce over the pasta and arrange the sliced duck in a fan shape on top of it. Garnish with raspberries and parsley and serve immediately.

Rigatoni & Pesto Baked Partridge

Partridge has a more delicate flavor than many game birds and this subtle sauce perfectly complements it.

Serves 4

INGREDIENTS

8 partridge pieces
  (about 4 ounces each)
4 tbsp butter, melted
4 tbsp Dijon mustard

2 tbsp lime juice
1 tbsp brown sugar
6 tbsp pesto sauce (see page 12)
1 pound dried rigatoni

1 tbsp olive oil
1$^1/_3$ cups freshly grated Parmesan
  cheese
salt and pepper

1 Arrange the partridge pieces, smooth side down, in a single layer in a large, ovenproof dish.

2 Mix together the butter, Dijon mustard, lime juice, and brown sugar in a bowl. Season to taste with salt and pepper. Brush this mixture over the uppermost surfaces of the partridge pieces and bake in a preheated oven at 400°F for 15 minutes.

3 Remove the dish from the oven and coat the partridge pieces with 3 tbsp of the pesto

sauce. Return to the oven and bake for a further 12 minutes.

4 Remove the dish from the oven and carefully turn over the partridge pieces. Coat the top of the partridges with the remaining mustard mixture and return to the oven for a further 10 minutes.

5 Meanwhile, bring a large saucepan of lightly salted water to a boil. Add the rigatoni and olive oil and cook for about 10 minutes, until tender, but still firm to the bite. Drain and transfer

to a large serving dish. Toss the pasta with the remaining pesto sauce and the Parmesan cheese.

6 Arrange the pieces of partridge on the serving dish with the rigatoni, pour the cooking juices on top, and serve immediately.

VARIATION

You could also prepare young pheasant in the same way.

Breast of Pheasant Lasagne with Baby Onions & Green Peas

This scrumptious and unusual baked lasagne is virtually a meal in itself.

Serves 4

INGREDIENTS

butter, for greasing
14 sheets precooked lasagne
3³/4 cups béchamel sauce (see page 166)
³/4 cup grated mozzarella cheese

FILLING:
8 ounces pork fat, diced
2 tbsp butter
16 small onions
8 large pheasant breasts, thinly sliced

¹/4 cup all-purpose flour
2¹/2 cups chicken stock
bouquet garni
1 pound fresh peas, shelled
salt and pepper

1 To make the filling, put the pork fat into a pan of boiling, salted water and simmer for 3 minutes, then drain, and pat dry.

2 Melt the butter in a large skillet. Add the pork fat and onions and cook for 3 minutes, until lightly browned.

3 Remove the pork fat and onions from the pan and set aside. Add the slices of pheasant and cook over a low heat for

12 minutes, until browned all over. Transfer to an ovenproof dish.

4 Stir the flour into the pan and cook until just brown, then blend in the stock. Pour over the pheasant, add the bouquet garni, and cook in a preheated oven at 400°F for 5 minutes.

5 Remove the bouquet garni. Add the onions, pork fat, and peas and return to the oven for 10 minutes.

6 Put the pheasant breasts and pork in a food processor and grind finely.

7 Lower the oven temperature to 375°F. Lightly grease an ovenproof dish with butter. Make layers of lasagne, pheasant sauce, and béchamel sauce in the dish, ending with béchamel sauce. Sprinkle with the cheese and bake in the oven for 30 minutes. Serve surrounded by the peas and onions.

Fish & Seafood

Pasta is a natural partner for fish and seafood. Both are cooked quickly to preserve their flavor and texture, they are packed full of nutritional goodness, and the varieties available are almost infinite. The superb recipes in this chapter demonstrate the full range of these qualities. For a quick, easy, and satisfying supper, try Spaghetti al Tonno, Casserole of Fusilli & Smoked Haddock with Egg Sauce, Seafood Lasagne, or Macaroni and Shrimp Bake. More unusual and sophisticated dishes include Sea Bass with Olive Sauce on a Bed of Macaroni, Poached Salmon Steaks with Penne, Farfallini Buttered Lobster, and Baked Scallops with Pasta in Shells. There are dishes to suit all tastes—freshwater and sea fish, shellfish and other seafood—and to suit all pockets. All are easy to make; the only problem is choosing which one to cook next.

Cannelloni Filetti di Sogliola

This is a lighter dish than the better-known cannelloni stuffed with ground beef.

Serves 6

INGREDIENTS

12 small fillets of sole
(about 4 ounces each)
$5/8$ cup red wine
6 tbsp butter
$3^{7}/8$ cups sliced
button mushrooms
4 shallots, finely chopped

4 ounces tomatoes, chopped
2 tbsp tomato paste
$1/2$ cup all-purpose
flour, sifted
$5/8$ cup warm milk
2 tbsp heavy cream
6 dried cannelloni tubes

6 ounces cooked, peeled shrimp,
preferably freshwater
salt and pepper
1 fresh fennel sprig, to garnish

1 Brush the fillets with a little wine, season with salt and pepper, and roll them up, skin side inward. Secure with a skewer or toothpick.

2 Arrange the fish rolls in a single layer in a large skillet, add the remaining red wine, and poach for about 4 minutes. Remove from the skillet and reserve the cooking liquid.

3 Melt the butter in another pan. Sauté the mushrooms and shallots for 2 minutes, then add the tomatoes and tomato paste. Season the flour and stir it into the pan. Stir in the reserved cooking liquid and half the milk. Cook over a low heat, stirring, for 4 minutes. Remove from the heat and stir in the cream.

4 Bring a large saucepan of lightly salted water to a boil. Add the cannelloni and cook for about 8 minutes, until tender but still firm to the bite. Drain and set aside to cool.

5 Remove the skewers or toothpicks from the fish rolls. Put 2 sole fillets into each cannelloni tube with 2–3 shrimp and a little red wine sauce. Arrange the cannelloni in an ovenproof dish, pour over the sauce and bake in a preheated oven at 400°F for 20 minutes.

6 Transfer the cannelloni to individual serving plates and serve with the red wine sauce, garnished with the remaining shrimp and a sprig of fennel.

Sea Bass with Olive Sauce on a Bed of Macaroni

A favorite fish for chefs, the delicious sea bass is now becoming increasingly common in supermarkets and fish stores for family meals.

Serves 4

INGREDIENTS

1 pound dried macaroni
1 tbsp olive oil
8 x 4 ounce sea bass medallions

TO GARNISH:
lemon slices
shredded leek
shredded carrot

SAUCE:
2 tbsp butter
4 shallots, chopped
2 tbsp capers
1$^{1}/_{2}$ cups pitted green olives, chopped
4 tbsp balsamic vinegar
1$^{1}/_{4}$ cups fish stock

1$^{1}/_{4}$ cups heavy cream
juice of 1 lemon
salt and pepper

1 To make the sauce, melt the butter in a skillet. Add the shallots and cook over a low heat for 4 minutes. Add the capers and olives and cook for a further 3 minutes.

2 Stir in the balsamic vinegar and fish stock, bring to a boil, and reduce by half. Add the cream, stirring, and reduce again by half. Season to taste with salt and pepper and stir in the lemon juice. Remove the pan from the heat, set aside and keep warm.

3 Bring a large saucepan of lightly salted water to a boil. Add the pasta and olive oil and cook for about 12 minutes, until tender but still firm to the bite.

4 Meanwhile, lightly broil the sea bass medallions for 3–4 minutes on each side, until cooked through, but still moist and delicate.

5 Drain the pasta thoroughly and transfer to a large serving dish. Top the pasta with the fish medallions and then pour on the olive sauce. Garnish with a few lemon slices, shredded leek, and shredded carrot and serve immediately.

Spaghetti alla Bucaniera

Brill was once known as poor man's turbot, an unfair description
as it is a delicately flavored and delicious fish in its own right.

Serves 4

INGREDIENTS

³/₄ cup all-purpose flour
1 pound brill or sole fillets, skinned
  and chopped
1 pound hake fillets, skinned
  and chopped
6 tbsp butter
4 shallots, finely chopped
2 garlic cloves, crushed

1 carrot, diced
1 leek, finely chopped
1¼ cups hard cider
1¼ cups medium sweet cider
2 tsp anchovy extract
1 tbsp tarragon vinegar
1 pound dried spaghetti
1 tbsp olive oil

salt and pepper
chopped fresh parsley, to garnish
crusty brown bread, to serve

1 Season the flour with salt and pepper to taste. Sprinkle ¼ cup of the seasoned flour onto a shallow plate. Press the fish pieces into the seasoned flour to coat thoroughly.

2 Melt the butter in a flameproof casserole. Add the fish fillets, shallots, garlic, carrot, and leek and cook over a low heat, stirring frequently, for about 10 minutes.

3 Sprinkle with the remaining seasoned flour and cook, stirring constantly, for 2 minutes. Gradually stir in the cider, anchovy extract, and tarragon vinegar. Bring to a boil and simmer over a low heat for 35 minutes. Alternatively, bake in a preheated oven at 350°F for 30 minutes.

4 About 15 minutes before the end of the cooking time, bring a large pan of lightly salted water to a boil. Add the spaghetti and olive oil and cook for about 12 minutes, until tender but still firm to the bite. Drain the spaghetti thoroughly and transfer to a large serving dish.

5 Arrange the fish on top of the spaghetti and cover with the sauce. Garnish with chopped parsley and serve immediately with warm, crusty brown bread.

Steamed Pasta Pudding

A tasty mixture of creamy fish and pasta cooked in a bowl, unmolded,
and drizzled with tomato sauce presents macaroni in a new guise.

Serves 4

INGREDIENTS

1 cup dried short-cut macaroni or
   other short pasta
1 tbsp olive oil
1 tbsp butter, plus extra for greasing
1 pound white fish fillets, such as
   cod or haddock
2–3 fresh parsley sprigs

6 black peppercorns
$1/2$ cup heavy cream
2 eggs, separated
2 tbsp chopped fresh dill or parsley
pinch of freshly grated nutmeg
$2/3$ cup freshly grated Parmesan
   cheese

salt and pepper
fresh dill or parsley sprigs, to garnish
tomato sauce (see page 54), to serve

1 Bring a pan of salted water to a boil. Add the pasta and olive oil and cook until tender, but still firm to the bite. Drain the pasta, return to the pan, add the butter, cover, and keep warm.

2 Place the fish in a skillet. Add the parsley sprigs, peppercorns, and enough water to cover. Bring to a boil, cover, and simmer for 10 minutes. Lift out the fish and set aside to cool. Reserve the cooking liquid.

3 Skin the fish and cut into bite-size pieces. Put the pasta in a bowl. Mix the cream, egg yolks, chopped dill or parsley, nutmeg, and cheese, pour into the pasta, and mix. Spoon in the fish without breaking it. Add enough of the reserved cooking liquid to make a moist, but firm mixture. Whisk the egg whites until stiff, then fold them into the mixture.

4 Grease a heatproof bowl and spoon in the fish mixture to

within $1\frac{1}{2}$ inches of the rim. Cover the top with greased baking paper and foil and tie securely with string.

5 Stand the bowl on a trivet in a saucepan. Add boiling water to reach halfway up the sides. Cover and steam for $1\frac{1}{2}$ hours.

6 Invert the pudding onto a serving plate. Pour over a little tomato sauce. Garnish and serve with the remaining tomato sauce.

Red Mullet Fillets with Orecchiette, Amaretto, & Orange Sauce

This succulent fish and pasta dish is ideal for serving on a warm, summer's evening—preferably al fresco.

Serves 4

INGREDIENTS

³/₄ cup all-purpose flour
8 red mullet fillets
2 tbsp butter
⁵/₈ cup fish stock
1 tbsp crushed almonds
1 tsp pink peppercorns
1 orange, peeled and cut
   into segments

1 tbsp orange liqueur
grated rind of 1 orange
1 pound dried orecchiette
1 tbsp olive oil
⁵/₈ cup heavy cream
4 tbsp amaretto
salt and pepper

TO GARNISH:
2 tbsp snipped fresh chives
1 tbsp toasted almonds

1 Season the flour with salt and pepper and sprinkle into a shallow bowl. Press the fish fillets into the flour to coat. Melt the butter in a skillet. Add the fish and fry over a low heat for 3 minutes, until browned.

2 Add the fish stock to the pan and cook for 4 minutes. Carefully remove the fish, cover with foil, and keep warm.

3 Add the almonds, pink peppercorns, half the orange, the orange liqueur, and orange rind to the pan. Simmer until the liquid has reduced by half.

4 Meanwhile, bring a large saucepan of lightly salted water to a boil. Add the orecchiette and olive oil and cook for 15 minutes, until tender but still firm to the bite.

5 Meanwhile, season the sauce with salt and pepper and stir in the cream and amaretto. Cook for 2 minutes. Return the fish to the pan to coat with the sauce.

6 Drain the pasta and transfer to a serving dish. Top with the fish fillets and their sauce. Garnish with the remaining orange segments, the chives, and toasted almonds. Serve immediately.

Vermicelli with Fillets of Red Mullet

*This simple recipe perfectly complements
the sweet flavor and delicate texture of the fish.*

Serves 4

INGREDIENTS

2¼ pounds red mullet fillets
1¼ cups dry white wine
4 shallots, finely chopped
1 garlic clove, crushed
3 tbsp finely chopped mixed
  fresh herbs

finely grated rind and juice of
  1 lemon
pinch of freshly grated nutmeg
3 anchovy fillets, roughly chopped
2 tbsp heavy cream
1 tsp cornstarch
1 pound dried vermicelli

1 tbsp olive oil
salt and pepper

TO GARNISH:
1 fresh mint sprig
lemon slices
lemon rind

1 Put the red mullet fillets in a large casserole. Pour the wine over and add the shallots, garlic, chopped herbs, lemon rind and juice, nutmeg, and anchovies. Season to taste with salt and pepper. Cover and bake in a preheated oven at 350°F for 35 minutes.

2 Carefully transfer the mullet to a warm dish. Set aside and keep warm while you prepare the sauce and pasta.

3 Pour the cooking liquid into a pan and bring to a boil. Simmer for 25 minutes, until reduced by half. Mix together the cream and cornstarch and stir into the sauce to thicken.

4 Meanwhile, bring a large pan of lightly salted water to a boil. Add the vermicelli and olive oil and cook for 8–10 minutes, until tender, but still firm to the bite. Drain the pasta and transfer to a warm serving dish.

5 Arrange the red mullet fillets on top of the vermicelli and pour the sauce over it. Garnish with a fresh mint sprig, slices of lemon, and strips of lemon rind and serve immediately.

COOK'S TIP

The best red mullet is sometimes called golden mullet, although it is bright red in color.

Spaghetti al Tonno

The classic Italian combination of pasta and tuna is enhanced in this recipe with a delicious parsley sauce.

Serves 4

INGREDIENTS

7 ounce can tuna, drained
2 ounce can anchovies, drained
1$\frac{1}{8}$ cups olive oil

1 cup roughly chopped parsley
$\frac{5}{8}$ cup crème fraîche
1 pound dried spaghetti
2 tbsp butter

salt and pepper
black olives, to garnish
crusty bread, to serve

1 Remove any bones from the tuna. Put the tuna into a food processor or blender, together with the anchovies, 1 cup of the olive oil, and the parsley. Process until the sauce is smooth.

2 Spoon the crème fraîche into the food processor or blender and process again for a few seconds to blend thoroughly. Season to taste with salt and black pepper.

3 Bring a large pan of lightly salted water to a boil. Add the spaghetti and the remaining olive oil and cook until tender, but still firm to the bite.

4 Drain the spaghetti, return to the saucepan and place over a medium heat. Add the butter and toss well to coat. Spoon in the sauce and quickly toss into the spaghetti, using 2 forks, until well combined.

5 Remove the saucepan from the heat and divide the spaghetti between 4 warm individual plates. Garnish with the olives and serve immediately with warm, crusty bread.

VARIATION

If desired, you could add 1–2 garlic cloves to the sauce, substitute ½ cup chopped fresh basil for half the parsley, and garnish with capers instead of black olives.

Casserole of Fusilli & Smoked Haddock with Egg Sauce

This quick, easy, and inexpensive dish would be ideal for a midweek family supper.

Serves 4

INGREDIENTS

2 tbsp butter, plus extra
   for greasing
1 pound smoked haddock fillets, cut
   into 4 slices
2¹/₂ cups milk
¹/₄ cup all-purpose flour
pinch of freshly grated nutmeg

3 tbsp heavy cream
1 tbsp chopped fresh parsley
2 eggs, hard cooked and mashed
   to a pulp
4 cups dried fusilli
1 tbsp lemon juice
salt and pepper

boiled new potatoes and beets,
   to serve

1 Thoroughly grease a casserole with butter. Put the haddock in the casserole and pour in the milk. Bake in a preheated oven at 400°F for about 15 minutes. Carefully pour the cooking liquid into a pitcher without breaking up the fish.

2 Melt the butter in a saucepan and stir in the flour. Gradually whisk in the reserved cooking liquid. Season to taste with salt, pepper, and nutmeg. Stir in the cream, parsley, and mashed egg and cook, stirring constantly, for 2 minutes.

3 Meanwhile, bring a large saucepan of lightly salted water to a boil. Add the fusilli and lemon juice and cook until tender, but still firm to the bite.

4 Drain the pasta and spoon or tip it over the fish. Top with the sauce and return the casserole to the oven for 10 minutes.

5 Serve immediately in the casserole with boiled new potatoes and beets.

VARIATION

You can use any type of dried pasta for this casserole. Try penne, conchiglie, or rigatoni.

Ravioli of Lemon Sole & Haddock

This delicate-tasting dish is surprisingly satisfying for even the hungriest appetites.

Serves 4

INGREDIENTS

1 pound lemon sole fillets, skinned
1 pound haddock fillets, skinned
3 eggs beaten
1 pound cooked potato gnocchi (see page 58)

3 cups fresh breadcrumbs
$^1/_4$ cup heavy cream
1 pound Basic Pasta Dough (see page 4)

$1^1/_4$ cups Italian red wine sauce (see page 52)
$^2/_3$ cup freshly grated Parmesan cheese
salt and pepper

1 Flake the lemon sole and haddock fillets with a fork and transfer the flesh to a large mixing bowl.

2 Mix the eggs, cooked potato gnocchi, breadcrumbs, and cream in a bowl until thoroughly combined. Add the fish to the bowl containing the gnocchi and season the mixture to taste with salt and black pepper.

3 Roll out the pasta dough on a lightly floured counter and cut out 3-inch rounds using a plain cutter.

4 Place a spoonful of the fish stuffing on each round. Dampen the edges slightly and fold the pasta rounds over, pressing together to seal.

5 Bring a large saucepan of lightly salted water to a boil. Add the ravioli and cook for 15 minutes.

6 Transfer the ravioli, using a slotted spoon, to a large serving dish. Pour the Italian red wine sauce over the ravioli, sprinkle with the Parmesan cheese, and serve immediately.

COOK'S TIP

When making square ravioli, divide the dough into two. Wrap half in plastic wrap and thinly roll out the other half. Cover with a clean, damp dish cloth while you roll out the remaining dough. Spoon or pipe the filling at regular intervals and brush the spaces in between with water or beaten egg. Lift the second sheet of dough into position with a rolling pin and press firmly between the filling to seal and expel any air. Cut out the shapes with a ravioli cutter or a sharp knife.

Poached Salmon Steaks with Penne

Fresh salmon and pasta in a mouthwatering lemon and watercress sauce—a wonderful summer evening treat.

Serves 4

INGREDIENTS

4 x 10 ounce fresh salmon steaks
4 tbsp butter
3/4 cup dry white wine
sea salt
8 peppercorns
fresh dill sprig
fresh tarragon sprig
1 lemon, sliced
1 pound dried penne

2 tbsp olive oil
lemon slices and fresh watercress,
    to garnish

LEMON & WATERCRESS SAUCE:
2 tbsp butter
1/4 cup all-purpose flour
5/8 cup warm milk

juice and finely grated rind of
    2 lemons
2 ounces watercress, chopped
salt and pepper

1 Put the salmon in a large, nonstick pan. Add the butter, wine, a pinch of sea salt, the peppercorns, dill, tarragon, and lemon. Cover, bring to a boil, and simmer for 10 minutes.

2 Using a fish slice, remove the salmon. Strain and reserve the cooking liquid. Remove and discard the salmon skin and center bones. Place the fish on a warm dish, cover, and keep warm.

3 Meanwhile, bring a saucepan of salted water to a boil. Add the penne and 1 tbsp of the oil and cook for 12 minutes, until tender but still firm to the bite. Drain and sprinkle with the remaining olive oil. Place on a warm serving dish, top with the salmon steaks, and keep warm.

4 To make the sauce, melt the butter and stir in the flour for 2 minutes. Stir in the milk and

about 7 tbsp of the reserved cooking liquid. Add the lemon juice and rind and cook, stirring, for a further 10 minutes.

5 Add the watercress to the sauce, stir gently, and season to taste with salt and pepper.

6 Pour the sauce over the salmon and penne, garnish with slices of lemon and fresh watercress, and serve immediately.

Spaghetti with Smoked Salmon

*Made in moments, this is a luxurious dish
to astonish and delight unexpected guests.*

Serves 4

INGREDIENTS

1 pound dried buckwheat spaghetti
2 tbsp olive oil
1/2 cup crumbled feta cheese
salt
fresh cilantro or parsley leaves,
   to garnish

SAUCE:
1 1/4 cups heavy cream
5/8 cup whiskey or brandy
4 1/2 ounces smoked salmon

pinch of cayenne pepper
black pepper
2 tbsp chopped fresh cilantro
   or parsley

1 Bring a large pan of lightly salted water to a boil. Add the spaghetti and 1 tbsp of the olive oil and cook until tender, but still firm to the bite. Drain the spaghetti, return to the pan, and sprinkle with the remaining olive oil. Cover, shake the pan, set aside, and keep warm.

2 Pour the cream into a small saucepan and bring to simmering point, but do not let it boil. Pour the whiskey or brandy into another small saucepan and bring to simmering point, but do not allow it to boil. Remove both pans from the heat and mix together the cream and whiskey or brandy.

3 Cut the smoked salmon into thin strips and add to the cream mixture. Season to taste with cayenne and black pepper. Just before serving, add the chopped fresh cilantro or parsley and stir until well combined.

4 Transfer the spaghetti to a warm serving dish, pour the sauce on, and toss thoroughly with 2 large forks. Scatter the crumbled feta cheese over the top, garnish with the cilantro or parsley leaves, and serve immediately.

COOK'S TIP

*Serve this rich and luxurious dish
with a green salad tossed in a
lemony dressing.*

Trout with Pasta Colle Acciughe & Smoked Bacon

*Most trout available nowadays is farmed rainbow trout,
however, if you can, buy wild brown trout for this recipe.*

Serves 4

INGREDIENTS

butter, for greasing
4 x 9¹/₂ ounce trout, gutted
   and cleaned
12 anchovies in oil, drained
   and chopped
2 apples, peeled, cored, and sliced

4 fresh mint sprigs
juice of 1 lemon
12 slices bacon
1 pound dried tagliatelle
1 tbsp olive oil
salt and pepper

TO GARNISH:
2 apples, cored and sliced
4 fresh mint sprigs

1 Grease a deep cookie sheet with butter.

2 Open up the cavities of each trout and wash thoroughly with warm salt water.

3 Season each cavity with salt and black pepper. Divide the anchovies, sliced apples, and mint sprigs between each of the cavities. Sprinkle the lemon juice into each cavity.

4 Carefully wrap each trout with three slices of bacon, covering all of the fish except for the head and tail.

5 Arrange the trout on the cookie sheet with the loose ends of bacon tucked neatly underneath. Season with black pepper to taste and bake in a preheated oven at 400°F for 20 minutes, turning the trout over after 10 minutes.

6 Meanwhile, bring a large pan of lightly salted water to a boil. Add the tagliatelle and olive oil and cook for about 12 minutes, until tender, but still firm to the bite. Drain the pasta and transfer to a large, warm serving dish.

7 Remove the trout from the oven and arrange on the tagliatelle. Garnish with sliced apples and fresh mint sprigs and serve immediately.

Farfalle with a Medley of Seafood

You can use almost any kind of sea fish in this recipe.
Red sea bream is an especially good choice.

Serves 4

INGREDIENTS

1 pound fillet of sea bream
4 tbsp butter
12 scallops, shelled
12 raw tiger shrimp
12 raw shrimp
4 1/2 ounces freshwater shrimp
juice and finely grated rind of
   1 lemon

pinch of saffron powder or threads
4 cups vegetable stock
5/8 cup rose petal vinegar (see
   page 98)
1 pound dried farfalle
1 tbsp olive oil
5/8 cup white wine
1 tbsp pink peppercorns

4 ounces baby carrots
5/8 cup heavy cream or fromage frais
salt and pepper

1 Peel and devein all of the shrimp. Thinly slice the sea bream. Melt the butter in a pan, add the sea bream, scallops, and shrimp, and cook for about 1–2 minutes.

2 Season with black pepper. Add the lemon juice and grated rind. Very carefully add a pinch of saffron powder or a few strands of saffron to the cooking juices (not to the seafood).

3 Remove the seafood from the pan, set aside and keep warm. Retain the juices.

4 Return the pan to the heat and add the vegetable stock. Bring to a boil and reduce by one-third. Add the vinegar and cook for 4 minutes, until reduced.

5 Bring a pan of salted water to a boil. Add the farfalle and olive oil and cook until tender, but still firm to the bite. Drain the pasta, transfer to a warm plate and top with the seafood.

6 Add the wine, peppercorns, and carrots to the pan and reduce the sauce for 6 minutes. Add the cream or fromage frais and simmer for 2 minutes.

7 Pour the sauce over the seafood and pasta and serve immediately.

Seafood Lasagne

This is one of those recipes where you can use any fish and any sauce you like: from smoked finnan haddock with a little whiskey sauce to cod with cheese sauce.

Serves 4

INGREDIENTS

1 pound finnan haddock, filleted, skin removed and flesh flaked

4 ounces shrimp

4 ounces sole fillet, skin removed and flesh sliced

juice of 1 lemon

4 tbsp butter

3 leeks, very thinly sliced

$1/2$ cup all-purpose flour

$2^1/3$ cups milk

2 tbsp clear honey

$1^3/4$ cups grated mozzarella cheese

1 pound precooked lasagne

$2/3$ cup freshly grated Parmesan cheese

black pepper

---

1 Put the haddock fillet, shrimp, and sole fillet into a large bowl and season with black pepper to taste and a little lemon juice. Set aside while you start to make the sauce.

2 Melt the butter in a large saucepan. Add the leeks and cook, stirring occasionally, for 8 minutes. Add the flour and cook, stirring constantly, for 1 minute. Gradually stir in enough milk to make a thick, creamy sauce.

3 Blend in the honey and mozzarella cheese and cook for a further 3 minutes. Remove the pan from the heat and mix in the fish and shrimp.

4 Make alternate layers of fish sauce and lasagne in an ovenproof dish, finishing with a layer of fish sauce on top. Generously sprinkle the grated Parmesan cheese and bake in a preheated oven at 350°F for 30 minutes. Serve the lasagne immediately.

VARIATION

For a cider sauce, substitute 1 finely chopped shallot for the leeks, 1¼ cups cider, and 1¼ cups heavy cream for the milk and 1 tsp mustard for the honey. For a Tuscan sauce, substitute 1 finely chopped fennel bulb for the leeks and omit the honey.

Spaghetti with Seafood Sauce

Peeled shrimp from the freezer can become the star ingredient in this colorful and tasty dish.

Serves 4

INGREDIENTS

8 ounces dried spaghetti, broken into 6-inch lengths
2 tbsp olive oil
1¼ cups chicken stock
1 tsp lemon juice
1 small cauliflower, cut into florets
2 carrots, thinly sliced
14 ounces snow peas

4 tbsp butter
1 onion, sliced
8 ounces zucchini, sliced
1 garlic clove, chopped
12 ounces frozen, cooked, peeled shrimp, defrosted
2 tbsp chopped fresh parsley

⅓ cup freshly grated Parmesan cheese
½ tsp paprika
salt and pepper
4 unpeeled, cooked shrimp, to garnish

1 Bring a pan of lightly salted water to a boil. Add the spaghetti and 1 tbsp of the olive oil and cook until tender, but still firm to the bite. Drain the spaghetti and return to the pan. Toss with the remaining olive oil, cover, and keep warm.

2 Bring the chicken stock and lemon juice to a boil. Add the cauliflower and carrots and cook for 3–4 minutes. Remove from the pan and set aside. Add the snow peas to the pan and cook for 1–2 minutes. Set aside with the other vegetables.

3 Melt half of the butter in a skillet set over a medium heat. Add the onion and zucchini to the skillet and sauté for about 3 minutes. Add the garlic and shrimp to the skillet and cook for a further 2–3 minutes, until thoroughly heated through.

4 Stir in the reserved vegetables and heat through. Season to taste with salt and pepper and stir in the remaining butter.

5 Transfer the spaghetti to a warm serving dish. Pour the sauce over the top and add the parsley. Toss well with 2 forks until thoroughly coated. Sprinkle with the Parmesan cheese and paprika, garnish with the unpeeled shrimp, and serve immediately.

Macaroni & Shrimp Bake

This adaptation of an eighteenth-century Italian dish is baked until it is golden brown and sizzling, then cut into wedges like a cake.

Serves 4

INGREDIENTS

3 cups dried short-cut macaroni

1 tbsp olive oil, plus extra
  for brushing

6 tbsp butter, plus extra for greasing

2 small fennel bulbs, thinly sliced and
  fronds reserved

6 ounces mushrooms, thinly sliced

6 ounces peeled, cooked shrimp

pinch of cayenne pepper

1¼ cups béchamel sauce (see
  Cook's Tip)

²/₃ cup freshly grated
  Parmesan cheese

2 large tomatoes, sliced

1 tsp dried oregano

salt and pepper

1 Bring a saucepan of salted water to a boil. Add the pasta and oil and cook until tender, but still firm to the bite. Drain and return to the pan. Add 2 tbsp of butter, cover, shake the pan, and keep warm.

2 Melt the remaining butter in a saucepan. Sauté the fennel for 3–4 minutes. Stir in the mushrooms and cook for a further 2 minutes. Stir in the shrimp, then remove the pan from the heat.

3 Stir the cayenne pepper and shrimp mixture into the béchamel sauce. Pour into a greased ovenproof dish and spread evenly. Sprinkle with the Parmesan cheese and arrange the tomato slices in a ring around the edge. Brush the tomatoes with olive oil and lightly sprinkle the oregano on top.

4 Bake in a preheated oven at 350°F for 25 minutes, until golden brown. Serve immediately.

COOK'S TIP

For béchamel sauce, melt 2 tbsp butter. Stir in ¼ cup flour. Cook, stirring, for 2 minutes. Gradually, stir in 1¼ cups warm milk. Add 2 tbsp finely chopped onion, 5 white peppercorns, and 2 parsley sprigs, and season with salt, dried thyme, and grated nutmeg. Simmer, stirring, for 15 minutes. Strain before using.

Pasta Packets

This is the ideal dish when you have guests because the packets can be prepared in advance and simply put in the oven when you are ready to eat.

Serves 4

INGREDIENTS

1 pound dried fettuccine
$^5/_8$ cup pesto sauce (see page 12)
4 tsp extra virgin olive oil

1 pound 10 ounces large raw shrimp, peeled and deveined
2 garlic cloves, crushed

$^1/_2$ cup dry white wine
salt and pepper

1 Cut out 4 x 12-inch squares of baking paper.

2 Bring a large saucepan of lightly salted water to a boil. Add the fettuccine and cook for 2–3 minutes, until just softened. Drain thoroughly, keep warm and set aside.

3 Mix together the fettuccine and half of the pesto sauce. Spread out the paper squares and put 1 tsp olive oil in the middle of each. Divide the fettuccine between the squares, then divide the shrimp, and place on top of the fettuccine.

4 Mix together the remaining pesto sauce and the garlic and spoon it over the shrimp. Season each packet with salt and black pepper and sprinkle with the white wine.

5 Dampen the edges of the baking paper and wrap the packets loosely, twisting the edges to seal.

6 Place the packets on a cookie sheet and bake in a preheated oven at 400°F for 10–15 minutes. Transfer the packets to 4 warm individual plates and serve immediately.

COOK'S TIP

Traditionally, these packets are designed to look like old-fashioned money bags. The resemblance is more effective with baking paper than with foil.

Farfallini Buttered Lobster

This is one of those dishes that looks almost too lovely to eat—but you should!

Serves 4

INGREDIENTS

2 x 1 pound 9 ounce lobsters, split
   into halves
juice and grated rind of 1 lemon
$\frac{1}{2}$ cup butter
4 tbsp fresh white breadcrumbs
2 tbsp brandy

5 tbsp heavy cream
   or crème fraîche
1 pound dried farfallini
1 tbsp olive oil
$\frac{2}{3}$ cup freshly grated
   Parmesan cheese
salt and pepper

TO GARNISH:
1 kiwi fruit, sliced
4 large, unpeeled, cooked shrimp
fresh dill sprigs

---

1 Carefully discard the stomach sac, vein, and gills from each lobster. Remove all the meat from the tail and chop. Crack the claws and legs, remove the meat, and chop. Transfer the meat to a bowl and add the lemon juice and grated lemon rind.

2 Clean the shells thoroughly and place in a warm oven at 325° to dry out.

3 Melt 2 tbsp of the butter in a skillet. Add the breadcrumbs and fry for about 3 minutes, until crisp and golden brown.

4 Melt the remaining butter in a saucepan. Add the lobster meat and heat through gently. Add the brandy and cook for a further 3 minutes, then add the cream or crème fraîche, and season to taste with salt and black pepper.

5 Meanwhile, bring a large pan of lightly salted water to a boil. Add the farfallini and olive oil and cook for about 12 minutes, until tender, but still firm to the bite. Drain thoroughly and spoon the pasta into the clean lobster shells. Top with the buttered lobster and sprinkle with a little grated Parmesan cheese and the breadcrumbs. Broil for 2–3 minutes, until a light golden brown color.

6 Transfer the lobster shells to a warm serving dish, garnish with the lemon slices, kiwi fruit, unpeeled shrimp, and dill sprigs and serve immediately.

Pasta Shells with Mussels

Serve this aromatic seafood dish to family and friends who admit to a love of garlic.

Serves 4–6

INGREDIENTS

$2^3/4$ pounds mussels
1 cup dry white wine
2 large onions, chopped
$1/2$ cup unsalted butter

6 large garlic cloves, finely chopped
5 tbsp chopped fresh parsley
$1^1/4$ cups heavy cream
14 ounces dried pasta shells

1 tbsp olive oil
salt and pepper
crusty bread, to serve

---

1 Scrub and debeard the mussels under cold running water. Discard any that do not close immediately when sharply tapped. Put the mussels into a large saucepan, together with the wine and half of the onions. Cover and cook over a medium heat, shaking the pan frequently, until the shells open.

2 Remove the pan from the heat. Drain the mussels and reserve the cooking liquid. Discard any mussels that have not opened. Strain the cooking liquid through a clean cloth into a glass pitcher or bowl and reserve.

3 Melt the butter in a pan over a medium heat. Add the remaining onion and sauté until translucent. Stir in the garlic and cook for 1 minute. Gradually stir in the reserved cooking liquid. Stir in the parsley and cream and season to taste with salt and black pepper. Bring to simmering point over a low heat.

4 Meanwhile, bring a large saucepan of lightly salted water to a boil. Add the pasta and olive oil and cook until just tender, but still firm to the bite. Drain the pasta, return to the pan, cover and keep warm.

5 Reserve a few mussels for the garnish and remove the remainder from their shells. Stir the shelled mussels into the cream sauce and warm briefly.

6 Transfer the pasta to a large, warm serving dish. Pour the sauce over the pasta and toss to coat. Garnish with the reserved mussels and serve with bread.

COOK'S TIP

Pasta shells are ideal because the sauce collects in the cavities and impregnates the pasta with flavor.

Saffron Mussel Tagliatelle

*Saffron is the most expensive spice in the world, but you only ever need
a small quantity. Saffron threads or powdered saffron may be used in this recipe.*

Serves 4

INGREDIENTS

2^1/$_4$ pounds mussels
^{5}/$_8$ cup white wine
1 medium onion, finely chopped
2 tbsp butter
2 garlic cloves, crushed
2 tsp cornstarch

1^1/$_4$ cups heavy cream
pinch of saffron threads or
    saffron powder
1 egg yolk
juice of ^{1}/$_2$ lemon
1 pound dried tagliatelle

1 tbsp olive oil
salt and pepper
3 tbsp chopped fresh parsley,
    to garnish

1 Scrub and debeard the mussels under cold running water. Discard any that do not close when sharply tapped. Put the mussels in a pan with the wine and onion. Cover and cook over a high heat, shaking the pan frequently, until the shells open.

2 Drain and reserve the cooking liquid. Discard any mussels that are still closed. Reserve a few mussels for the garnish and remove the remainder from their shells.

3 Strain the cooking liquid into a saucepan. Bring to a boil and reduce by about half. Remove the pan from the heat.

4 Melt the butter in a saucepan. Add the garlic and cook, stirring frequently, for 2 minutes, until golden brown. Stir in the cornstarch and cook, stirring, for 1 minute. Gradually stir in the cooking liquid and the cream. Crush the saffron threads and add to the pan. Season with salt and pepper to taste and simmer over a

low heat for 2–3 minutes, until the sauce has thickened.

5 Stir in the egg yolk, lemon juice, and shelled mussels. Do not allow the mixture to boil.

6 Meanwhile, bring a pan of salted water to a boil. Add the pasta and oil and cook until tender, but still firm to the bite. Drain and transfer to a serving dish. Add the mussel sauce and toss. Garnish with the parsley and reserved mussels and serve.

Baked Scallops with Pasta in Shells

This is another tempting seafood dish where the eye is delighted as much as the taste buds.

Serves 4

INGREDIENTS

12 scallops
3 tbsp olive oil
3 cups small, dried whole-wheat
   pasta shells
$^5/_8$ cup fish stock
1 onion, chopped

juice and finely grated rind of
   2 lemons
$^5/_8$ cup heavy cream
2 cups freshly grated
   cheddar cheese

salt and pepper
crusty brown bread, to serve

---

1 Remove the scallops from their shells. Scrape off the skirt and the black intestinal thread. Reserve the white part (the flesh) and the orange part (the coral or roe). Very carefully ease the flesh and coral from the shell with a short, but very strong knife.

2 Wash the shells thoroughly and dry them well. Put the shells on a cookie sheet, sprinkle lightly with about two-thirds of the olive oil, and set aside.

3 Meanwhile, bring a large saucepan of lightly salted water to a boil. Add the pasta shells and remaining olive oil and cook for about 12 minutes, until tender, but still firm to the bite. Drain and spoon about 1 ounce of pasta into each scallop shell.

4 Put the scallops, fish stock, and onion in an ovenproof dish and season to taste with pepper. Cover with foil and bake in a preheated oven at 350°F for 8 minutes.

5 Remove the dish from the oven. Remove the foil and, using a slotted spoon, transfer the scallops to the shells. Add 1 tbsp of the cooking liquid to each shell, together with a drizzle of lemon juice and a little cream, and top with the grated cheese.

6 Increase the oven temperature to 450°F and return the scallops to the oven for a further 4 minutes.

7 Serve the scallops in their shells with crusty brown bread and butter.

Vermicelli with Clams

A quickly cooked recipe that transforms
cupboard ingredients into a dish with style.

Serves 4

INGREDIENTS

14 ounces dried vermicelli, spaghetti,
  or other long pasta
2 tbsp olive oil
2 tbsp butter
2 onions, chopped

2 garlic cloves, chopped
2 x 7 ounce jars clams in brine
1/2 cup white wine
4 tbsp chopped fresh parsley
1/2 tsp dried oregano

pinch of freshly grated nutmeg
salt and pepper

TO GARNISH:
2 tbsp Parmesan cheese shavings
fresh basil sprigs

1 Bring a large pan of lightly salted water to a boil. Add the pasta and half the olive oil and cook until tender, but still firm to the bite. Drain, return to the pan, and add the butter. Cover the pan, shake well, and keep warm.

2 Heat the remaining oil in a pan over a medium heat. Add the onions and sauté until they are translucent. Stir in the garlic and cook for 1 minute.

3 Strain the liquid from 1 jar of clams and add the liquid to the pan, with the wine. Stir, bring to simmering point, and simmer for 3 minutes. Drain the second jar of clams and discard the liquid.

4 Add the clams, parsley, and oregano to the pan and season with pepper and nutmeg. Lower the heat and cook until the sauce is heated through.

5 Transfer the pasta to a warm serving dish and pour the sauce over the top. Sprinkle with the Parmesan cheese, garnish with the basil, and serve immediately.

COOK'S TIP

There are many different types of clams found along almost every coast in the world. Those traditionally used in this dish are the very tiny ones—only 1–2 inches across—known in Italy as vongole.

Squid & Macaroni Stew

*This scrumptious seafood dish is quick and
easy to make, yet deliciously satisfying to eat.*

Serves 4–6

INGREDIENTS

2 cups dried short-cut macaroni
  or other small pasta shapes
7 tbsp olive oil
2 onions, sliced
12 ounces prepared squid, cut into
  1^1/$_2$-inch strips

1 cup fish stock
^{5}/$_8$ cup red wine
12 ounces tomatoes, skinned and
  thinly sliced
2 tbsp tomato paste
1 tsp dried oregano

2 bay leaves
2 tbsp chopped fresh parsley
salt and pepper
crusty bread, to serve

1 Bring a large saucepan of lightly salted water to a boil. Add the pasta and 1 tbsp of the olive oil and cook for 3 minutes. Drain, return to the pan, cover, and keep warm.

2 Heat the remaining oil in a pan over a medium heat. Add the onions and sauté until they are translucent. Add the squid and stock and simmer for 5 minutes. Pour in the wine and add the tomatoes, tomato paste, oregano, and bay leaves. Bring the sauce to a boil, season to taste, and cook for 5 minutes.

3 Stir the pasta into the pan, cover, and simmer for about 10 minutes, or until the squid and macaroni are tender and the sauce has thickened. If the sauce remains too liquid, uncover the pan and continue cooking for a few minutes.

4 Remove and discard the bay leaves. Reserve a little parsley and stir the remainder into the pan. Transfer to a warm serving dish and sprinkle with the remaining parsley. Serve with crusty bread to soak up the sauce.

COOK'S TIP

To prepare squid, peel off the outer skin, then cut off the head and tentacles. Extract the transparent flat oval bone from the body and discard. Remove the sac of black ink, then turn the body sac inside out. Wash in cold water. Cut off the tentacles and discard the rest; wash thoroughly.

Vegetables & Salads

The pasta recipes in this chapter offer something special for every occasion: filling vegetarian suppers, unusual vegetable side dishes, main courses, and side salads. You could even take many of the salads on a picnic and, of course, they are perfect as accompaniments for summer barbecues. Some are classic dishes, such as Fettuccine all'Alfredo, Spaghetti Olio e Aglio, Paglia e Fieno, and Pasta & Herring Salad. Others are imaginative and sometimes surprising new combinations of vegetables and pasta. Try Mediterranean Spaghetti, Spinach & Wild Mushroom Lasagne, Ravioli with Vegetable Stuffing, and Rare Beef Pasta Salad for a family meal, while Linguine with Braised Fennel, Goat's Cheese with Penne & Walnut Salad, and Pasta & Garlic Mayo Salad make superb side dishes to get the taste buds tingling.

Fettuccine all'Alfredo

This simple, traditional dish can be made with any long pasta,
but is especially good with flat noodles, such as fettuccine or tagliatelle.

Serves 4

INGREDIENTS

2 tbsp butter
⅞ cup heavy cream
1 pound fresh fettuccine
1 tbsp olive oil

1 cup freshly grated Parmesan
cheese, plus extra
to serve

pinch of freshly grated nutmeg
salt and pepper
fresh parsley sprigs, to garnish

1 Put the butter and ⅝ cup of the cream in a large saucepan and bring the mixture to a boil over a medium heat. Reduce the heat and then simmer gently for about 1½ minutes, or until slightly thickened.

2 Meanwhile, bring a large saucepan of lightly salted water to a boil. Add the fettuccine and olive oil and cook for 2–3 minutes, until tender, but still firm to the bite. Drain the fettuccine thoroughly and then pour the cream and butter sauce over the top.

3 Toss the fettuccine in the sauce over a low heat until thoroughly coated.

4 Add the remaining cream, the Parmesan cheese, and nutmeg to the fettuccine mixture and season to taste with salt and pepper. Toss thoroughly to coat while gently heating through.

5 Transfer the fettuccine mixture to a warm serving plate and garnish with the fresh sprig of parsley. Serve immediately, with extra grated Parmesan cheese on the side.

VARIATION

This classic Roman dish is often served with the addition of strips of ham and fresh peas. Add 2 cups shelled cooked peas and 6 ounces ham strips with the Parmesan cheese in step 4.

Macaroni Bake

This satisfying dish would make an
excellent supper for a midweek family meal.

Serves 4

INGREDIENTS

4 cups dried short-cut macaroni
1 tbsp olive oil
4 tbsp beef drippings
1 pound potatoes, thinly sliced

1 pound onions, sliced
2 cups grated mozzarella
cheese
$^5/_8$ cup heavy cream

salt and pepper
crusty brown bread and butter, to serve

1 Bring a large saucepan of lightly salted water to a boil. Add the macaroni and olive oil and cook for about 12 minutes, until tender, but still firm to the bite. Drain the macaroni thoroughly and set aside.

2 Melt the drippings in a large flameproof casserole, then remove from the heat.

3 Make alternate layers of potatoes, onions, macaroni, and grated cheese in the dish, seasoning well with salt and pepper to taste between each layer and finishing with a layer of cheese on top. Finally, pour the cream over the top layer of cheese.

4 Bake in a preheated oven at 400°F for 25 minutes. Remove the dish from the oven and carefully brown the top under a broiler.

5 Serve hot straight from the dish, with lots of crusty brown bread and butter, as a main course. Alternatively, you could serve the dish as a vegetable accompaniment with your favorite main course.

VARIATION

For a stronger flavor, use mozzarella affumicata, *a smoked version of this cheese, or Swiss cheese instead of the mozzarella.*

Creamy Pasta & Broccoli

This colorful dish provides a mouthwatering contrast in the crisp "al dente" texture of the broccoli and the creamy cheese sauce.

Serves 4

INGREDIENTS

4 tbsp butter
1 large onion, finely chopped
1 pound dried ribbon pasta
1 pound broccoli, broken into florets

$^5/_8$ cup boiling vegetable stock
1 tbsp all-purpose flour
$^5/_8$ cup light cream
$^1/_2$ cup grated mozzarella cheese
freshly grated nutmeg

salt and white pepper
fresh apple slices, to garnish

1 Melt half of the butter in a large saucepan over a medium heat. Add the onion and sauté for 4 minutes.

2 Add the broccoli and pasta to the pan and cook, stirring constantly, for 2 minutes. Add the vegetable stock, bring back to a boil, and simmer for a further 12 minutes. Season well with salt and white pepper.

3 Meanwhile, melt the remaining butter in a saucepan over a medium heat.

Sprinkle in the flour and cook, stirring constantly, for 2 minutes. Gradually stir in the cream and bring to simmering point, but do not boil. Add the grated cheese and season with salt and a little freshly grated nutmeg.

4 Drain the pasta and broccoli mixture and pour in the cheese sauce. Cook, stirring occasionally, for about 2 minutes. Transfer the pasta and broccoli mixture to a warm, large, deep serving dish, and serve garnished with slices of fresh apple.

VARIATION

This dish would also be delicious and look just as colorful made with Cape broccoli, which is actually a purple variety of cauliflower and not broccoli at all.

Paglia e Fieno

The name of this dish—"straw and hay"—
refers to the colors of the pasta when mixed together.

Serves 4

INGREDIENTS

4 tbsp butter
1 pound fresh peas, shelled
$7/8$ cup heavy cream

1 pound mixed fresh green and white
    spaghetti or tagliatelle
1 tbsp olive oil

$2/3$ cup freshly grated Parmesan
    cheese, plus extra to serve
pinch of freshly grated nutmeg
salt and pepper

1 Melt the butter in a large saucepan. Add the peas and cook, over a low heat, for 2–3 minutes.

2 Using a measuring pitcher, pour $5/8$ cup of the cream into the pan, bring to a boil, and simmer for 1–1½ minutes, until slightly thickened. Remove the pan from the heat.

3 Meanwhile, bring a large pan of lightly salted water to a boil. Add the spaghetti or tagliatelle and olive oil and cook for 2–3 minutes, until just tender,

but still firm to the bite. Remove the pan from the heat, drain the pasta thoroughly, and return to the pan.

4 Add the peas and cream sauce to the pasta. Return the pan to the heat and add the remaining cream and the Parmesan cheese. Season to taste with salt, black pepper, and a pinch of grated nutmeg.

5 Using 2 forks, gently toss the pasta to coat with the peas and cream sauce, while it is heating through.

6 Transfer the pasta to a serving dish and serve immediately, with extra Parmesan cheese.

VARIATION

Sauté 2 cups sliced button or oyster mushrooms in 4 tbsp butter over a low heat for 4–5 minutes. Stir into the peas and cream sauce just before adding to the pasta in step 4.

Green Tagliatelle with Garlic

A rich pasta dish for garlic lovers everywhere.
It is quick and easy to prepare and full of flavor.

Serves 4

INGREDIENTS

2 tbsp walnut oil
1 bunch scallions, sliced
2 garlic cloves, thinly sliced
3¼ cups sliced mushrooms
1 pound fresh green and white
   tagliatelle
1 tbsp olive oil

8 ounces frozen spinach, thawed and
   drained
½ cup full-fat soft cheese with
   garlic and herbs
4 tbsp light cream
½ cup chopped, unsalted
   pistachio nuts
salt and pepper

TO GARNISH:
2 tbsp shredded fresh basil
fresh basil sprigs
Italian bread, to serve

1 Heat the walnut oil in a large skillet. Add the scallions and garlic and sauté for 1 minute, until just softened.

2 Add the mushrooms to the pan, stir well, cover, and cook over a low heat for about 5 minutes, until softened.

3 Meanwhile, bring a large saucepan of lightly salted water to a boil. Add the tagliatelle and olive oil and cook for 3–5 minutes, until tender, but still firm to the bite. Drain the tagliatelle thoroughly and return to the saucepan.

4 Add the spinach to the skillet and heat through for about 1–2 minutes. Add the cheese to the pan and allow to melt slightly. Stir in the cream and continue to cook, stirring occasionally and without allowing the mixture to come to a boil, until it is completely warmed through.

5 Pour the sauce over the pasta, season to taste with salt and black pepper, and mix well. Heat through gently, stirring constantly, for 2–3 minutes.

6 Transfer the pasta to a serving dish and sprinkle with the pistachio nuts and shredded basil. Garnish with the basil sprigs and serve immediately with the Italian bread of your choice.

Spaghetti Olio e Aglio

This easy and satisfying Roman dish originated as a cheap meal for poor people, but has now become a favorite in restaurants and trattorias.

Serves 4

INGREDIENTS

$^1/_2$ cup olive oil
3 garlic cloves, crushed

1 pound fresh spaghetti

3 tbsp roughly chopped fresh parsley
salt and pepper

1 Reserve 1 tbsp of the olive oil and heat the remainder in a medium saucepan. Add the garlic and a pinch of salt and cook over a low heat, stirring constantly, until golden brown, then remove the pan from the heat. Do not allow the garlic to burn as it will taint its flavor. (If it does burn, you will have to start all over again!)

2 Meanwhile, bring a large saucepan of lightly salted water to a boil. Add the spaghetti and remaining olive oil and cook for 2–3 minutes, until tender, but still firm to the bite. Drain the spaghetti thoroughly and return to the pan.

3 Add the oil and garlic mixture to the spaghetti and toss to coat thoroughly. Season with pepper, add the chopped fresh parsley, and toss to coat again.

4 Transfer the spaghetti to a warm serving dish and serve immediately.

COOK'S TIP

Oils produced by different countries, mainly Italy, Spain, and Greece, have their own characteristic flavors. Some produce an oil which has a hot, peppery taste while others have a "green" flavor.

COOK'S TIP

It is worth buying the best-quality olive oil for dishes such as this one which makes a feature of its flavor, and for salad dressings in addition. Extra virgin oil is produced from the first pressing and has the lowest acidity. It is more expensive than other types of olive oil, but has the finest flavor. Virgin olive oil is slightly more acid, but is also well flavored. Oil simply labeled pure has usually been heat-treated and refined by mechanical means and, consequently, lacks character and flavor.

Patriotic Pasta

*The ingredients of this dish have the same
bright colors as the Italian flag—hence its name.*

Serves 4

INGREDIENTS

4 cups dried farfalle

4 tbsp olive oil

1 pound cherry tomatoes

3 ounces arugula

salt and pepper

Pecorino cheese, to garnish

1 Bring a large saucepan of lightly salted water to a boil. Add the farfalle and 1 tbsp of the olive oil and cook until tender, but still firm to the bite. Drain the farfalle thoroughly and return to the pan.

2 Cut the cherry tomatoes in half and trim the arugula, using a sharp knife.

3 Heat the remaining olive oil in a large saucepan. Add the tomatoes and cook for 1 minute. Add the farfalle and the arugula and stir gently to mix. Heat through and season to taste with salt and black pepper.

4 Meanwhile, using a vegetable peeler, shave thin slices of Pecorino cheese.

5 Transfer the farfalle and vegetables to a warm serving dish. Garnish with the Pecorino cheese shavings and serve immediately.

COOK'S TIP

Pecorino cheese is a hard ewe's milk cheese which resembles Parmesan and is often used for grating over a variety of dishes. It has a sharp flavor and is used only in small quantities.

COOK'S TIP

Arugula is a small plant with irregular-shaped leaves rather like those of turnip greens. The flavor is distinctively peppery and slightly reminiscent of radish. It has always been popular in Italy, both in salads and for serving with pasta, and has recently enjoyed a revival in the United States and Britain.

Mediterranean Spaghetti

Delicious Mediterranean vegetables, cooked in rich tomato sauce,
make an ideal topping for nutty whole-wheat pasta.

Serves 4

INGREDIENTS

2 tbsp olive oil
1 large, red onion, chopped
2 garlic cloves, crushed
1 tbsp lemon juice
4 baby eggplants, quartered

2$\frac{1}{2}$ cups sieved tomatoes
2 tsp superfine sugar
2 tbsp tomato paste
14 ounce can artichoke hearts,
   drained and halved

1 cup pitted black olives
12 ounces dried spaghetti
2 tbsp butter
salt and pepper
fresh basil sprigs, to garnish
olive bread, to serve

1 Heat 1 tbsp of the olive oil in a large skillet. Add the onion, garlic, lemon juice, and eggplant and cook over a low heat for 4–5 minutes, until the onion and eggplant are lightly golden brown.

2 Pour in the sieved tomatoes, season to taste with salt and black pepper, and stir in the sugar and tomato paste. Bring to a boil, lower the heat, and then simmer, stirring occasionally, for about 20 minutes.

3 Gently stir in the artichoke hearts and black olives and cook for 5 minutes.

4 Meanwhile, bring a large saucepan of lightly salted water to a boil. Add the spaghetti and the remaining oil and cook for 7–8 minutes, until tender, but still firm to the bite.

5 Drain the spaghetti thoroughly and toss with the butter. Transfer to a serving dish.

6 Pour the vegetable sauce over the spaghetti, garnish with the sprigs of fresh basil, and serve immediately with olive bread.

Spinach & Mushroom Lasagne

This is one of the tastiest vegetarian dishes. Always check the seasoning of vegetables, as it is most important. You can always add a little more seasoning to a recipe, but you cannot take it out once it has been added.

Serves 4

INGREDIENTS

8 tbsp butter, plus extra for greasing

2 garlic cloves, finely chopped

4 ounces shallots

8 ounces exotic mushrooms, such as chanterelles

1 pound spinach, cooked, drained and finely chopped

2 cups grated cheddar cheese

1/4 tsp freshly grated nutmeg

1 tsp chopped fresh basil

2 ounces all-purpose flour

2 1/2 cups hot milk

2/3 cup grated Cheshire cheese

salt and pepper

8 sheets precooked lasagne

1 Lightly grease an ovenproof dish with a little butter.

2 Melt 4 tbsp of the butter in a saucepan. Add the garlic, shallots, and mushrooms and sauté over a low heat for 3 minutes. Stir in the spinach, cheddar cheese, nutmeg, and basil. Season well with salt and black pepper and set aside.

3 Melt the remaining butter in another saucepan over a low heat. Add the flour and cook, stirring constantly, for 1 minute. Gradually stir in the hot milk, whisking constantly until smooth. Stir in 1/4 cup of the Cheshire cheese and season to taste with salt and black pepper.

4 Spread half of the mushroom and spinach mixture over the base of the prepared dish. Cover with a layer of lasagne and then with half of the cheese sauce. Repeat the process and sprinkle

with the remaining Cheshire cheese. Bake in a preheated oven at 400°F for 30 minutes, until golden brown.

VARIATION

You could substitute 4 bell peppers for the spinach. Roast in a preheated oven at 400°F for 20 minutes. Rub off the skins under cold water, seed, and chop before using.

Ravioli with Vegetable Stuffing

It is important not to overcook the vegetable filling or it will become sloppy and unexciting, instead of firm to the bite and delicious.

Serves 4

INGREDIENTS

1 pound Basic Pasta Dough (see page 4)
1 tbsp olive oil
6 tbsp butter
⅝ cup light cream
1 cup freshly grated Parmesan cheese

STUFFING:
2 large eggplant
3 large zucchini
6 large tomatoes
1 large green bell pepper
1 large red bell pepper
3 garlic cloves
1 large onion

½ cup olive oil
2 ounces tomato paste
½ tsp chopped fresh basil
salt and pepper

1 To make the stuffing, cut the eggplant and zucchini into 1-inch chunks. Put the eggplant pieces in a colander, sprinkle with salt and set aside for 20 minutes. Rinse the eggplant and drain thoroughly.

2 Blanch the tomatoes in boiling water for 2 minutes. Drain, skin, and chop the flesh. Core and seed the bell peppers and cut into 1-inch pieces. Chop the garlic and onion.

3 Heat the oil in a saucepan. Add the garlic and onion and sauté for 3 minutes. Stir in the eggplant, zucchini, tomatoes, bell peppers, tomato paste, and basil. Season with salt and pepper to taste, cover, and leave to simmer for about 20 minutes, stirring frequently.

4 Roll out the pasta dough and cut out 3-inch rounds with a plain cutter. Put a spoonful of the vegetable stuffing onto each

round. Dampen the edges slightly and fold the pasta rounds over, pressing together to seal.

5 Bring a saucepan of salted water to a boil. Add the ravioli and the oil and cook for 3–4 minutes. Drain and transfer to a greased ovenproof dish, dotting each layer with butter. Pour in the cream and sprinkle with the Parmesan cheese. Bake in a preheated oven at 400°F for 20 minutes. Serve hot.

Zucchini & Eggplant Lasagne

This rich, baked pasta dish is packed full of vegetables, tomatoes, and Italian mozzarella cheese.

Serves 6

INGREDIENTS

2 ¼ pounds eggplant
8 tbsp olive oil
2 tbsp garlic and herb butter
1 pound zucchini, sliced
2 cups grated
   mozzarella cheese

2 ½ cups sieved tomatoes
6 sheets precooked green
   lasagne
2 ½ cups béchamel sauce (see
   page 166)

⅔ cup freshly grated
   Parmesan cheese
1 tsp dried oregano
salt and pepper

1 Thinly slice the eggplant and place in a colander. Sprinkle with salt and set aside for 20 minutes. Rinse and pat dry with paper towels.

2 Heat 4 tbsp of the olive oil in a large skillet. Fry half the eggplant slices over a low heat for 6–7 minutes, until golden. Drain on paper towels. Repeat with the remaining oil and eggplant slices.

3 Melt the garlic and herb butter in the skillet. Add the zucchini and fry for 5–6 minutes, until golden brown all over. Drain on paper towels.

4 Place half the eggplant and zucchini slices in a large ovenproof dish. Season with pepper and sprinkle with half the mozzarella cheese. Spoon half the sieved tomatoes over the cheese and top with 3 sheets of lasagne.

Repeat the process, ending with a layer of lasagne.

5 Top with the béchamel sauce and sprinkle the Parmesan cheese and oregano. Put the dish on a cookie sheet and bake in a preheated oven at 425°F for 30–35 minutes, until golden brown. Serve immediately.

Pasta & Bean Casserole

A satisfying winter dish, pasta and bean casserole with a crunchy topping is a slow-cooked, one-dish meal.

Serves 6

INGREDIENTS

1¼ cups dried navy beans, soaked overnight and drained

8 ounces dried penne

6 tbsp olive oil

3½ cups vegetable stock

2 large onions, sliced

2 garlic cloves, chopped

2 bay leaves

1 tsp dried oregano

1 tsp dried thyme

5 tbsp red wine

2 tbsp tomato paste

2 celery stalks, sliced

1 fennel bulb, sliced

1⅝ cups sliced mushrooms

8 ounces tomatoes, sliced

1 tsp dark muscovado sugar

4 tbsp dry white breadcrumbs

salt and pepper

salad greens and crusty bread, to serve

1 Put the navy beans in a large saucepan and add sufficient cold water to cover. Bring to a boil and continue to boil vigorously for 20 minutes. Drain, set aside, and keep warm.

2 Bring a large saucepan of lightly salted water to a boil. Add the penne and 1 tbsp of the olive oil and cook for about 3 minutes. Drain the pasta, set aside, and keep warm.

3 Put the beans in a large, flameproof casserole. Add the vegetable stock and stir in the remaining olive oil, the onions, garlic, bay leaves, oregano, thyme, wine, and tomato paste. Bring to a boil, then cover, and cook in a preheated oven at 350°F for 2 hours.

4 Add the penne, celery, fennel, mushrooms, and tomatoes to the casserole and season to taste with salt and pepper. Stir in the sugar and top with the breadcrumbs. Cover the dish and cook in the oven for 1 further hour.

5 Serve hot with salad greens and crusty bread.

Creamed Spaghetti & Mushrooms

*This easy vegetarian dish is ideal for busy people
with little time, but good taste!*

Serves 4

INGREDIENTS

4 tbsp butter

2 tbsp olive oil

6 shallots, sliced

6 cups sliced
   button mushrooms

1 tsp all-purpose flour

$^5/_8$ cup heavy cream

2 tbsp port

4 ounces sun-dried
   tomatoes, chopped

freshly grated nutmeg

1 pound dried spaghetti

1 tbsp freshly chopped parsley

salt and pepper

6 triangles of fried white bread,
   to serve

1 Heat the butter and 1 tbsp of the oil in a large saucepan. Add the shallots and cook over a medium heat for 3 minutes. Add the mushrooms and cook over a low heat for 2 minutes. Season with salt and black pepper, sprinkle in the flour, and cook, stirring constantly, for 1 minute.

2 Gradually stir in the cream and port, add the sun-dried tomatoes and a pinch of grated nutmeg, and cook over a low heat for 8 minutes.

3 Meanwhile, bring a large saucepan of lightly salted water to a boil. Add the spaghetti and remaining olive oil and cook for 12–14 minutes, until tender but still firm to the bite.

4 Drain the spaghetti and return to the pan. Add the mushroom sauce and cook for 3 minutes. Transfer the spaghetti and mushroom sauce to a large serving plate and sprinkle with chopped parsley. Serve with crispy triangles of fried bread.

VARIATION

Nonvegetarians could add 4 ounces prosciutto, cut into thin strips and heated gently in 2 tbsp butter, to the pasta along with the mushroom sauce.

Vegetable Pasta Stir-fry

*Prepare all the vegetables and cook the pasta in advance,
then the dish can be cooked in a few minutes.*

Serves 4

INGREDIENTS

14 ounces dried whole-wheat pasta
   shells or other short
   pasta shapes
1 tbsp olive oil
2 carrots, thinly sliced
4 ounces baby corncobs
3 tbsp corn oil
1-inch piece fresh ginger root,
   thinly sliced

1 large onion, thinly sliced
1 garlic clove, thinly sliced
3 celery stalks, thinly sliced
1 small red bell pepper, cored,
   seeded, and cut into
   matchstick strips
1 small green bell pepper, cored,
   seeded, and cut into
   matchstick strips

1 tsp cornstarch
2 tbsp water
3 tbsp soy sauce
3 tbsp dry sherry
1 tsp clear honey
a dash of hot pepper sauce (optional)
salt

1 Bring a large saucepan of lightly salted water to a boil. Add the pasta and olive oil and cook until tender, but still firm to the bite. Drain, return to the pan, and keep warm.

2 Bring a saucepan of lightly salted water to a boil. Add the carrots and corncobs and cook for 2 minutes. Drain, rinse in cold water, and drain again.

3 Heat the corn oil in a preheated wok or large skillet. Add the ginger root and stir-fry over a medium heat for 1 minute to flavor the oil. Remove the ginger from the oil with a slotted spoon and discard.

4 Add the onion, garlic, celery, and bell peppers to the wok or skillet and stir-fry for 2 minutes. Add the carrots and baby corncobs and stir-fry for a further 2 minutes. Stir in the drained pasta.

5 Mix together the cornstarch and water to make a smooth paste. Stir in the soy sauce, sherry, and honey. Pour the cornstarch mixture into the pasta and cook, stirring occasionally, for 2 minutes. Stir in a dash of pepper sauce, if liked. Transfer to a serving dish and serve immediately.

Macaroni & Corn Pancakes

This vegetable pancake can be filled with your favorite vegetables, as long as they are cooked beforehand. A favorite alternative is shredded parsnips with 1 tbsp mustard.

Serves 4

INGREDIENTS

2 corncobs
4 tbsp butter
4 ounces red bell peppers, cored,
    seeded, and finely diced
$2^{1}/_{2}$ cups dried short-
    cut macaroni

$^{5}/_{8}$ cup heavy cream
$^{1}/_{4}$ cup all-purpose flour
4 egg yolks
4 tbsp olive oil
salt and pepper

TO SERVE:
oyster mushrooms
fried leeks

1 Bring a saucepan of water to a boil, add the corncobs and cook for about 8 minutes. Drain thoroughly and rinse under cold running water for 3 minutes. Carefully cut away the kernels onto paper towels and set aside to dry.

2 Melt 2 tbsp of the butter in a skillet. Add the bell peppers and cook over a low heat, stirring occasionally, for 4 minutes. Drain thoroughly and pat dry with paper towels.

3 Bring a large pan of lightly salted water to a boil. Add the macaroni and cook for 12 minutes, until tender, but still firm to the bite. Drain the macaroni and leave to cool in cold water.

4 Beat together the cream, flour, a pinch of salt, and the egg yolks in a bowl until smooth. Add the corn and bell peppers to the cream and egg mixture. Drain the macaroni and toss into the corn and cream mixture. Season well with black pepper to taste.

5 Heat the remaining butter with the oil in a large skillet. Drop spoonfuls of the mixture into the pan and press down until the mixture forms a flat pancake. Fry until golden on both sides, and all the mixture is used up. Serve immediately with oyster mushrooms and fried leeks.

Vermicelli Flan

*Lightly cooked vermicelli is pressed into a flan ring
and baked with a creamy mushroom filling.*

Serves 4

INGREDIENTS

6 tbsp butter, plus extra,
   for greasing
8 ounces dried vermicelli or spaghetti
1 tbsp olive oil
1 onion, chopped
5 ounces button mushrooms

1 green bell pepper, cored, seeded,
   and sliced into thin rings
$5/8$ cup milk
3 eggs, lightly beaten
2 tbsp heavy cream
1 tsp dried oregano

freshly grated nutmeg
1 tbsp freshly grated
   Parmesan cheese
salt and pepper
tomato and basil salad, to serve

1 Generously grease the base and sides of an 8-inch loose-based flan pan with butter.

2 Bring a large pan of lightly salted water to a boil. Add the vermicelli and olive oil and cook until tender, but still firm to the bite. Drain, return to the pan, add 2 tbsp of the butter and shake the pan to coat the pasta.

3 Press the pasta onto the base and around the sides of the flan pan to make a flan case.

4 Melt the remaining butter in a skillet over a medium heat. Add the onion and sauté until it is translucent.

5 Add the mushrooms and bell pepper rings to the skillet and cook, stirring and turning constantly, for 2–3 minutes. Spoon the onion, mushroom and bell peppers into the flan case and press down evenly over the base.

6 Beat together the milk, eggs, and cream, stir in the oregano, and season to taste with nutmeg and black pepper. Carefully pour the mixture over the vegetables and sprinkle with the cheese.

7 Bake the flan in a preheated oven at 350°F for 40–45 minutes, until the filling has set.

8 Slide the flan out of the pan and serve warm with a tomato and basil salad.

Fettuccine with Olive, Garlic, & Walnut Sauce

This mouthwatering dish would make an excellent light, vegetarian lunch for four or a good starter for six.

Serves 4–6

INGREDIENTS

2 thick slices whole-wheat bread, crusts removed
1¼ cups milk
2½ cups shelled walnuts
2 garlic cloves, crushed

1 cup pitted black olives
²/₃ cup freshly grated Parmesan cheese
8 tbsp extra virgin olive oil
⁵/₈ cup heavy cream

1 pound fresh fettuccine
salt and pepper
2–3 tbsp chopped fresh parsley

1 Put the bread in a shallow dish, pour the milk over it, and set aside to soak until the liquid has been absorbed.

2 Spread the walnuts out on a cookie sheet and toast in a preheated oven at 375°F for about 5 minutes, until golden. Set aside to cool.

3 Put the soaked bread, walnuts, garlic, olives, Parmesan cheese, and 6 tbsp of the olive oil in a food processor and purée. Season to taste with a little salt and black pepper and stir in the cream.

4 Bring a large pan of lightly salted water to a boil. Add the fettuccine and 1 tablespoon of the remaining oil and cook for 2–3 minutes, until tender but still firm to the bite. Drain the fettuccine thoroughly and toss with the remaining olive oil, until well combined.

5 Divide the fettuccine between individual plates and spoon the olive, garlic, and walnut sauce on top. Sprinkle with the fresh parsley and serve.

COOK'S TIP

Parmesan quickly loses its pungency and "bite." It is better to buy small quantities and grate it yourself. Wrapped in foil, it will keep in the refrigerator for several months.

Linguine with Braised Fennel

*This aniseed-flavored vegetable gives that
extra punch to this delicious creamy pasta dish.*

Serves 4

INGREDIENTS

6 fennel bulbs
⁵/₈ cup vegetable stock
2 tbsp butter
6 slices bacon, diced
6 shallots, quartered

¹/₄ cup all-purpose flour
7 tbsp heavy cream
1 tbsp Madeira

1 pound dried linguine
1 tbsp olive oil
salt and pepper

1 Trim the fennel bulbs, then gently peel off and reserve the first layer of the bulbs. Cut the bulbs into quarters and put them in a large saucepan, together with the vegetable stock and the reserved outer layers. Bring to a boil, lower the heat, and simmer for 5 minutes.

2 Using a slotted spoon, transfer the fennel to a large dish. Discard the outer layers of the fennel bulb. Bring the vegetable stock to a boil and allow to reduce by half. Set aside.

3 Melt the butter in a skillet. Add the bacon and shallots and fry for 4 minutes. Add the flour, reduced stock, cream, and Madeira and cook, stirring constantly, for 3 minutes, until the sauce is smooth. Season to taste with salt and black pepper and pour over the fennel.

4 Bring a large saucepan of lightly salted water to a boil. Add the linguine and olive oil and cook for 10 minutes, until tender, but still firm to the bite. Drain and transfer to a deep ovenproof dish.

5 Add the fennel and sauce and braise in a preheated oven at 350°F for 20 minutes. Serve immediately from the dish.

COOK'S TIP

Fennel will keep in the salad drawer of the refrigerator for 2–3 days, but it is best eaten as fresh as possible. Cut surfaces turn brown quickly, so do not prepare it too much in advance of cooking.

Baked Eggplant with Pasta

Combined with tomatoes and mozzarella cheese, pasta
makes a tasty filling for baked eggplant shells.

Serves 4

INGREDIENTS

8 ounces dried penne or other short
  pasta shapes
4 tbsp olive oil, plus extra for
  brushing
2 eggplant

1 large onion, chopped
2 garlic cloves, crushed
14 ounce can chopped tomatoes
2 tsp dried oregano
2 ounces mozzarella cheese,
  thinly sliced

$^1/_3$ cup freshly grated
  Parmesan cheese
2 tbsp dry breadcrumbs
salt and pepper
salad greens, to serve

1 Bring a saucepan of lightly salted water to a boil. Add the pasta and 1 tbsp of the olive oil and cook until tender, but still firm to the bite. Drain, return to the pan, cover, and keep warm.

2 Cut the eggplant in half lengthwise and score around the inside with a sharp knife, being careful not to pierce the shells. Scoop out the flesh with a spoon. Brush the insides of the shells with olive oil. Chop the flesh and set aside.

3 Heat the remaining oil in a skillet. Sauté the onion until translucent. Add the garlic and cook for 1 minute. Add the chopped eggplant and cook, stirring frequently, for 5 minutes. Add the tomatoes and oregano and season to taste with salt and pepper. Bring to a boil and simmer for 10 minutes, or until thickened. Remove from the heat and stir in the pasta.

4 Brush a cookie sheet with oil and arrange the eggplant

shells in a single layer. Divide half the tomato and pasta mixture between them. Sprinkle the mozzarella on, then pile the remaining tomato and pasta mixture on top. Mix the Parmesan cheese and breadcrumbs together and sprinkle over the top, patting it lightly into the tomato and pasta mixture.

5 Bake in a preheated oven at 400°F for 25 minutes, until the topping is golden brown. Serve hot with salad greens.

Pasta with Green Vegetable Sauce

The different shapes and textures of the vegetables make a mouthwatering presentation in this light and summery dish.

Serves 4

INGREDIENTS

2 cups dried gemelli or other
   pasta shapes
1 tbsp olive oil
1 head green broccoli, cut
   into florets
2 zucchini, sliced

8 ounces asparagus spears
4 ounces snow peas
4 ounces frozen peas
2 tbsp butter
3 tbsp vegetable stock
4 tbsp heavy cream

freshly grated nutmeg
2 tbsp chopped fresh parsley
2 tbsp freshly grated
   Parmesan cheese
salt and pepper

1 Bring a large saucepan of lightly salted water to a boil. Add the pasta and olive oil and cook until tender, but still firm to the bite. Drain, return to the pan, cover, and keep warm.

2 Steam the broccoli, zucchini, asparagus spears, and snow peas over a pan of boiling salted water until they are just beginning to soften. Remove from the heat and rinse in cold water. Drain thoroughly, and set aside until required.

3 Bring a small pan of lightly salted water to a boil. Add the frozen peas and cook for 3 minutes. Drain the peas, rinse in cold water, and then drain again. Set aside with the other vegetables.

4 Put the butter and vegetable stock in a pan over a medium heat. Add all of the vegetables, reserving a few of the asparagus spears, and toss carefully with a wooden spoon until they have heated through, taking care not to break them up.

5 Stir in the cream and heat through without bringing to a boil. Season to taste with salt, pepper, and nutmeg.

6 Transfer the pasta to a warmed serving dish and stir in the chopped parsley. Spoon the vegetable sauce on top and sprinkle with Parmesan cheese. Arrange the reserved asparagus spears in a pattern on top and serve.

Niçoise with Pasta Shells

This is a more filling variation on the traditional
Niçoise salad from southern France.

Serves 4

INGREDIENTS

12 ounces dried small pasta shells
1 tbsp olive oil
4 ounces green beans
1³/₄ ounce can anchovies, drained
¹/₈ cup milk
2 small crisp lettuce heads

1 pound or 3 large beef tomatoes
4 hard-cooked eggs
8 ounce can tuna, drained
1 cup pitted black olives
salt and pepper

VINAIGRETTE DRESSING:
¹/₄ cup extra virgin olive oil
¹/₈ cup white wine vinegar
1 tsp wholegrain mustard
salt and pepper

1 Bring a large saucepan of lightly salted water to a boil. Add the pasta and the olive oil and cook until tender, but still firm to the bite. Drain and rinse in cold water.

2 Bring a small saucepan of lightly salted water to a boil. Add the beans and cook for 10–12 minutes, until tender, but still firm to the bite. Drain, rinse in cold water, drain thoroughly once more, and then set aside.

3 Put the anchovies in a shallow bowl, cover with the milk, and set aside for 10 minutes. Meanwhile, tear the lettuce into large pieces. Blanch the tomatoes in boiling water for 1–2 minutes, then drain, skin, and roughly chop the flesh. Shell the eggs and cut into quarters. Cut the tuna into large chunks.

4 Drain the anchovies and the pasta. Put all of the salad ingredients, the beans, and the olives into a large bowl and gently mix together.

5 To make the vinaigrette dressing, beat together all the dressing ingredients and keep in the refrigerator until required. Just before serving, pour the vinaigrette dressing over the salad.

COOK'S TIP

It is very convenient to make salad dressings in a screw top jar. Put all the ingredients in the jar, cover securely, and shake well to mix and emulsify the oil.

Herring & Pasta Salad

This salad, which so many countries claim as their own,
is also considered in Holland to be a typically Dutch dish.

Serves 4

INGREDIENTS

9 ounces dried pasta shells

5 tbsp olive oil

14 ounces rollmop herrings in brine

6 boiled potatoes

2 large tart apples

2 baby frisée lettuces

2 baby beets

4 hard-cooked eggs

6 pickled onions

6 dill pickles

2 tbsp capers

3 tbsp tarragon vinegar

salt and pepper

1 Bring a large saucepan of lightly salted water to a boil. Add the pasta and 1 tbsp of the olive oil and cook until tender, but still firm to the bite. Drain the pasta thoroughly and rinse in cold water.

2 Cut the herrings, potatoes, apples, frisée lettuces, and beets into small pieces. Put all of these ingredients into a large salad bowl.

3 Drain the pasta thoroughly and add to the salad bowl.

Toss lightly to mix the pasta and herring mixture together.

4 Carefully shell and slice the eggs. Garnish the salad with the slices of egg, pickled onions, dill pickles, and capers, sprinkle with the remaining olive oil and the tarragon vinegar, and serve immediately.

COOK'S TIP

Store this salad, without the dressing,
in a container in the refrigerator.

COOK'S TIP

Tarragon vinegar is available from most supermarkets, but you can easily make your own. Add a bunch of fresh tarragon to a bottle of white or red wine vinegar and leave to infuse for 48 hours. It is important to ensure that the tarragon is as fresh as possible and to discard any blemished leaves.

Neapolitan Seafood Salad with Campanelle

This delicious mix of seafood, salad greens, and ripe tomatoes conjures up all the warmth and sunshine of Naples.

Serves 4

INGREDIENTS

1 pound prepared squid, cut into strips
1 pound 10 ounces cooked mussels
1 pound cooked cockles in brine
$5/8$ cup white wine

$1^1/4$ cups olive oil
2 cups dried campanelle or other small pasta shapes
juice of 1 lemon
1 bunch chives, snipped

1 bunch fresh parsley, finely chopped
4 large tomatoes, quartered or sliced
mixed salad greens
salt and pepper
sprig of fresh basil, to garnish

1 Put all of the seafood into a large bowl, pour in the wine and half the olive oil, and set aside for 6 hours.

2 Put the seafood mixture into a saucepan and simmer over a low heat for 10 minutes. Set aside to cool.

3 Bring a large saucepan of lightly salted water to a boil. Add the pasta and 1 tbsp of the remaining olive oil and cook until tender, but still firm to the bite. Drain thoroughly and rinse in cold water.

4 Strain off about half of the cooking liquid from the seafood and discard the rest. Mix in the lemon juice, chives, parsley, and the remaining olive oil. Season to taste with salt and pepper. Drain the pasta and add to the seafood.

5 Slice or cut the tomatoes into quarters. Shred the salad greens and arrange them on the base of a salad bowl. Spoon in the seafood salad and garnish with the quartered or sliced tomatoes and a sprig of basil.

VARIATION

You can substitute cooked scallops for the mussels, and clams in brine for the cockles.

Pasta Salad with Red & White Cabbage

This crunchy, colorful salad would be a good accompaniment for broiled meat or fish.

Serves 4

INGREDIENTS

2¼ cups dried short-
  cut macaroni
5 tbsp olive oil
1 large red cabbage, shredded

1 large white cabbage, shredded
2 large apples, diced
9 ounces cooked smoked bacon or
  ham, diced

8 tbsp wine vinegar
1 tbsp sugar
salt and pepper

1 Bring a large saucepan of lightly salted water to a boil. Add the macaroni and 1 tablespoon of the olive oil and cook until tender, but still firm to the bite. Drain the pasta, then rinse in cold water. Drain the pasta again and set aside.

2 Bring a large saucepan of lightly salted water to a boil. Add the shredded red cabbage and cook for 5 minutes. Drain thoroughly and set aside to cool.

3 Bring a large saucepan of lightly salted water to a boil. Add the white cabbage and cook for 5 minutes. Drain thoroughly and set aside to cool.

4 In a large bowl, mix together the pasta, red cabbage, and apple. In a separate bowl, mix together the white cabbage and bacon or ham.

5 In a small bowl, mix together the remaining oil, the vinegar, and sugar and season to taste with salt and pepper. Pour the dressing over each of the 2 cabbage mixtures and, finally, mix them all together. Serve immediately.

VARIATION

Alternative dressings for this salad can be made with 4 tbsp olive oil, 4 tbsp red wine, 4 tbsp red wine vinegar, and 1 tbsp sugar. Or you could substitute 3 tbsp olive oil and 1 tbsp walnut or hazelnut oil for the olive oil.

Dolcelatte, Nut, & Pasta Salad

*Use colorful salad greens to provide visual contrast
to match the contrasts of taste and texture.*

Serves 4

INGREDIENTS

2 cups dried pasta shells
1 tbsp olive oil
1 cup shelled and halved walnuts
mixed salad greens, such
   as radicchio, escarole, arugula, corn
   salad, and frisée

8 ounces dolcelatte cheese, crumbled
salt

DRESSING:
2 tbsp walnut oil
4 tbsp extra virgin olive oil
2 tbsp red wine vinegar
salt and pepper

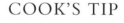

1 Bring a large saucepan of lightly salted water to a boil. Add the pasta shells and olive oil and cook until just tender, but still firm to the bite. Drain the pasta, rinse under cold running water, drain thoroughly again, and set aside.

2 Spread out the shelled walnut halves on a cookie sheet and toast under a preheated broiler for about 2–3 minutes. Set aside to cool slightly while you make the dressing.

3 To make the dressing, whisk together the walnut oil, olive oil, and vinegar in a small bowl, and season to taste with salt and black pepper.

4 Arrange the salad greens in a large serving bowl. Pile the cooled pasta in the middle of the salad greens and sprinkle the dolcelatte cheese on top. Pour the dressing over the pasta salad, scatter with the walnut halves and toss together well to mix. Serve immediately.

COOK'S TIP

Dolcelatte is a semisoft, blue-veined cheese from Italy. Its texture is creamy and smooth and the flavor is delicate, but piquant. You could substitute Roquefort as an alternative. Whichever cheese you choose, it is essential that it is of the best quality and in peak condition.

Goat's Cheese with Penne, Pear, & Walnut Salad

This superb salad was created especially to accompany venison cooked in Chablis, but is equally delicious with other strongly flavored meat dishes.

Serves 4

INGREDIENTS

9 ounces dried penne
5 tbsp olive oil
1 head radicchio, torn into pieces
1 Webbs lettuce, torn into pieces
7 tbsp chopped walnuts

2 ripe pears, cored and diced
1 fresh basil sprig
1 bunch of watercress, trimmed
2 tbsp lemon juice
3 tbsp garlic vinegar

4 tomatoes, quartered
1 small onion, sliced
1 large carrot, grated
9 ounces goat's cheese, diced
salt and pepper

1 Bring a large saucepan of lightly salted water to a boil. Add the penne and 1 tbsp of the olive oil and cook until tender, but still firm to the bite. Drain the pasta, rinse under cold running water, drain thoroughly again, and set aside to cool.

2 Place the radicchio and Webbs lettuce in a large salad bowl and mix together well. Top with the pasta, walnuts, pears, basil, and watercress.

3 Mix together the lemon juice, the remaining olive oil, and the vinegar in a pitcher. Pour the mixture over the salad ingredients and toss thoroughly to coat the salad greens well.

4 Add the tomato quarters, onion slices, grated carrot, and diced goat's cheese and toss together, using 2 forks, until well mixed. Leave the salad to chill in the refrigerator for about 1 hour before serving.

COOK'S TIP

Most goat's cheese comes from France and there are many varieties, such as Crottin de Chavignol, Chabi, which is very pungent, and Sainte-Maure, which is available in creamery and farmhouse varieties.

Pasta & Garlic Mayo Salad

This crisp salad would make an excellent accompaniment to broiled meat and is ideal for summer barbecues.

Serves 4

INGREDIENTS

2 large lettuce heads
9 ounces dried penne
1 tbsp olive oil
8 red delicious apples

juice of 4 lemons
1 head of celery, sliced
³/4 cup shelled, halved walnuts

1¹/8 cups fresh garlic mayonnaise
  (see Cook's Tip, below right)
salt

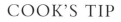

1 Wash, drain, and pat dry the lettuce leaves with paper towels. Transfer them to the refrigerator for 1 hour until crisp.

2 Meanwhile, bring a large saucepan of lightly salted water to a boil. Add the pasta and olive oil and cook until tender, but still firm to the bite. Drain the pasta and rinse under cold running water. Drain thoroughly again and set aside.

3 Core and dice the apples, place them in a small bowl, and sprinkle with the lemon juice.

Mix together the pasta, celery, apples, and walnuts and toss the mixture in the garlic mayonnaise (see Cook's Tip, right). Add more mayonnaise, if desired.

4 Line a salad bowl with the lettuce leaves and spoon the pasta salad into the lined bowl. Serve when required.

COOK'S TIP

Sprinkling the apples with lemon juice will prevent them from turning brown.

COOK'S TIP

To make homemade garlic mayonnaise, beat 2 egg yolks with a pinch of salt and 6 crushed garlic cloves. Start beating in 1½ cups olive oil, 1–2 tsp at a time, using a balloon whisk or electric mixer. When about one-quarter of the oil has been fully incorporated, beat in 1–2 tbsp white wine vinegar. Continue beating in the oil, adding it in a thin, continuous stream. Finally, stir in 1 tsp Dijon mustard and season to taste with salt and pepper.

Fusilli, Avocado, Tomato, & Mozzarella Salad

Tomatoes and mozzarella cheese are a classic Italian combination.
Here they are joined with pasta spirals and avocado for an extra touch of luxury.

Serves 4

INGREDIENTS

2 tbsp pine nuts
1¹/₂ cups dried fusilli
1 tbsp olive oil
6 tomatoes
8 ounces mozzarella cheese

1 large avocado
2 tbsp lemon juice
3 tbsp chopped fresh basil
salt and pepper
fresh basil sprigs, to garnish

DRESSING:
6 tbsp extra virgin olive oil
2 tbsp white wine vinegar
1 tsp wholegrain mustard
pinch of sugar

1 Spread the pine nuts out on a cookie sheet and toast under a preheated broiler for 1–2 minutes. Remove and set aside to cool.

2 Bring a large saucepan of lightly salted water to a boil. Add the fusilli and olive oil and cook until tender, but still firm to the bite. Drain the pasta and rinse in cold water. Drain the pasta again and then set aside to cool slightly.

3 Thinly slice the tomatoes and the mozzarella cheese.

4 Cut the avocado in half, remove the pit, and skin. Cut into thin slices lengthwise and sprinkle with lemon juice to prevent discoloration.

5 To make the dressing, whisk together the oil, vinegar, mustard, and sugar in a small bowl, and season to taste with salt and black pepper.

6 Arrange the tomatoes, mozzarella cheese, and avocado alternately in overlapping slices on a large serving platter.

7 Toss the pasta with half of the dressing and the chopped basil, and season to taste with salt and black pepper. Spoon the pasta into the center of the platter and pour the remaining dressing on top. Sprinkle with the pine nuts, garnish with fresh basil sprigs, and serve immediately.

Pasta-stuffed Tomatoes

*This unusual and inexpensive dish would make a good starter
for eight people or a delicious lunch for four.*

Serves 4

INGREDIENTS

5 tbsp extra virgin olive oil, plus extra
for greasing
8 beef tomatoes or large round
tomatoes

1 cup dried ditalini or other very
small pasta shapes
8 black olives, pitted and finely
chopped
2 tbsp finely chopped fresh basil

1 tbsp finely chopped fresh parsley
$2/3$ cup freshly grated
Parmesan cheese
salt and pepper
fresh basil sprigs, to garnish

---

1 Brush a cookie sheet with
olive oil.

2 Slice the tops off the
tomatoes and reserve to make
"lids." If the tomatoes will not
stand up, cut a thin slice off the
bottom of each tomato.

3 Using a teaspoon, scoop
out the tomato pulp into a
strainer, but do not pierce the
tomato shells. Invert the tomato
shells onto paper towels, pat dry,
and then set aside to drain
thoroughly.

4 Bring a large saucepan of
lightly salted water to a boil.
Add the ditalini or other pasta and
1 tbsp of the remaining olive oil
and cook until tender, but still firm
to the bite. Drain the pasta
thoroughly and set aside.

5 Put the olives, chopped basil,
parsley, and Parmesan cheese
into a large mixing bowl and stir in
the drained tomato pulp. Add the
pasta to the bowl. Stir in the
remaining olive oil, mix together
well, and season to taste with salt
and pepper.

6 Spoon the pasta mixture into
the tomato shells and replace
the lids. Arrange the tomatoes on
the cookie sheet and bake in a
preheated oven at 375°F for
15–20 minutes.

7 Remove the tomatoes from
the oven and allow to cool
until just warm. Arrange on a
serving dish, garnish with the basil
sprigs, and serve.

Rare Beef Pasta Salad

This salad is a meal in itself and would be perfect for an al fresco *lunch, perhaps with a bottle of red wine.*

Serves 4

INGREDIENTS

1 pound rump or sirloin steak in one piece
1 pound dried fusilli
5 tbsp olive oil
2 tbsp lime juice

2 tbsp Thai fish sauce (see Cook's Tip)
2 tsp clear honey
4 scallions, sliced
1 cucumber, peeled and cut into 1-inch chunks

3 tomatoes, cut into wedges
3 tsp finely chopped fresh mint
salt and pepper

1 Season the steak with salt and black pepper to taste. Broil or pan-fry the steak for 4 minutes on each side. Set aside for 5 minutes, then slice thinly across the grain.

2 Meanwhile, bring a large saucepan of lightly salted water to a boil. Add the fusilli and 1 tbsp of the olive oil and cook until tender, but still firm to the bite. Drain the fusilli, rinse in cold water, and drain again thoroughly. Toss the fusilli in the remaining olive oil.

3 Combine the lime juice, fish sauce, and honey in a small saucepan and cook over a medium heat for 2 minutes.

4 Add the scallions, cucumber, tomatoes, and mint to the pan, then add the sliced steak and mix thoroughly. Season to taste with salt.

5 Transfer the fusilli to a large, warm serving dish and top with the steak and salad mixture. Serve just warm or allow to cool completely first.

COOK'S TIP

Thai fish sauce, also known as nam pla, is made from salted anchovies and has quite a strong flavor, so it should be used with discretion. It is available from some supermarkets and from Oriental food stores.

Beet Cannolicchi

*Quick and simple, this colorful, warm salad works equally
well as a tasty starter or as a main dish.*

Serves 4

INGREDIENTS

11 ounces dried ditalini rigati
5 tbsp olive oil
2 garlic cloves, chopped
14 ounce can chopped tomatoes

14 ounces cooked beet, diced
2 tbsp chopped fresh basil leaves
1 tsp mustard seeds
salt and pepper

TO SERVE:
mixed salad greens, tossed in olive oil
4 Italian plum tomatoes, sliced

1 Bring a large saucepan of lightly salted water to a boil. Add the pasta and 1 tbsp of the oil and cook for about 10 minutes, until tender, but still firm to the bite. Drain the pasta thoroughly and set aside.

2 Heat the remaining olive oil in a large saucepan. Add the garlic and sauté for 3 minutes. Add the chopped tomatoes and cook for 10 minutes.

3 Remove the pan from the heat and carefully add the beet, basil, mustard seeds, and

pasta, and season to taste with salt and black pepper.

4 Serve on a bed of mixed salad greens tossed in olive oil, and sliced plum tomatoes.

COOK'S TIP

To cook raw beet, trim off the leaves about 2 inches above the root and ensure that the skin is not broken. Boil in very lightly salted water for 30–40 minutes, until tender. Leave to cool completely and then rub off the skin.

COOK'S TIP

Mustard seeds come from three different plants and may be black, brown, or white. Black and brown mustard seeds have a stronger, more pungent flavor than white mustard.

Desserts

If desserts do not usually spring to your mind when you think about cooking with pasta, you will be amazed by the wonderfully self-indulgent sweet treats in this chapter. Who could resist Honey & Walnut Nests, a scrumptious combination of pistachio nuts, honey, and crisp angel hair pasta? Raspberry Fusilli is a feast for the eyes as well as the taste buds, German Noodle Pudding is a rich and satisfying dessert based on a traditional Jewish recipe, and Baked Sweet Ravioli is a revelation to anyone with a sweet tooth. The recipes in this chapter will convince you that pasta desserts are much more exciting than a macaroni milk pudding, and your family and guests will be delighted with such imaginative ways to end a meal.

Baked Sweet Ravioli

These scrumptious little packets are the perfect
dessert for anyone with a really sweet tooth.

Serves 4

INGREDIENTS

PASTA:
3³/₄ cups all-purpose flour
10 tbsp butter, plus extra for greasing
³/₄ cup superfine sugar
4 eggs

1 ounce yeast
¹/₂ cup warm milk

FILLING:
²/₃ cup chestnut purée
¹/₂ cup cocoa powder
¹/₄ cup superfine sugar

¹/₂ cup chopped almonds
1 cup crushed amaretti cookies
⁵/₈ cup orange marmalade

1 To make the sweet pasta dough, sift the flour into a mixing bowl, then mix in the butter, sugar, and 3 eggs.

2 Mix together the yeast and warm milk in a small bowl and when thoroughly combined, mix into the dough.

3 Knead the dough for 20 minutes, cover with a clean cloth, and set aside in a warm place for 1 hour to rise.

4 Mix together the chestnut purée, cocoa powder, sugar, almonds, crushed amaretti cookies, and orange marmalade in a separate bowl.

5 Lightly grease a cookie sheet with butter.

6 Lightly flour the counter. Roll out the pasta dough into a thin sheet and then cut into 2-inch rounds with a plain pastry cutter.

7 Put a spoonful of filling onto each round and then fold in half, pressing the edges to seal. Arrange on the prepared cookie sheet, spacing the ravioli out well.

8 Beat the remaining egg and brush all over the ravioli to glaze. Bake in a preheated oven at 350°F for 20 minutes. Serve hot.

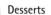

German Noodle Pudding

This rich and satisfying pudding is a traditional Jewish recipe.

Serves 4

INGREDIENTS

4 tbsp butter, plus extra
   for greasing
6 ounces ribbon egg noodles
1/2 cup cream cheese
1 cup cottage cheese
1/2 cup superfine sugar
2 eggs, lightly beaten

1/2 cup sour cream
1 tsp vanilla extract
a pinch of ground cinnamon
1 tsp grated lemon rind
1/4 cup slivered almonds
3/8 cup dry white breadcrumbs
confectioner's sugar, for dusting

1 Grease an ovenproof dish with butter.

2 Bring a large pan of water to a boil. Add the noodles and cook until almost tender. Drain and set aside.

3 Beat together the cream cheese, cottage cheese, and sugar in a mixing bowl. Beat in the eggs, a little at a time. Stir in the sour cream, vanilla extract, cinnamon, and lemon rind, and fold in the noodles. Transfer the mixture to the prepared dish and smooth the surface.

4 Melt the butter in a skillet. Add the almonds and fry, stirring constantly, for about 1–1½ minutes, until lightly colored. Remove the skillet from the heat and stir the breadcrumbs into the almonds.

5 Sprinkle the almond and breadcrumb mixture over the pudding and bake in a preheated oven at 350°F for about 35-40 minutes, until just set. Dust with a little confectioner's sugar and serve immediately.

VARIATION

Although not authentic, you could add 3 tbsp raisins with the lemon rind in step 3, if desired.

Honey & Walnut Nests

Pistachio nuts and honey are combined with crisp cooked angel hair pasta in this unusual Greek dessert.

Serves 4

INGREDIENTS

8 ounces angel hair pasta

8 tbsp butter

1¹/₂ cups shelled pistachio
   nuts, chopped

¹/₂ cup sugar

¹/₃ cup clear honey

⁵/₈ cup water

2 tsp lemon juice

salt

strained, plain yogurt, to serve

1 Bring a large saucepan of lightly salted water to a boil. Add the angel hair pasta and cook until tender, but still firm to the bite. Drain the pasta and return to the pan. Add the butter and toss to coat the pasta thoroughly. Set aside to cool.

2 Arrange 4 small flan or poaching rings on a cookie sheet. Divide the angel hair pasta into 8 equal quantities and spoon 4 of them into the rings. Press down lightly. Top the pasta with half of the nuts, then add the remaining pasta.

3 Bake in a preheated oven at 350°F for 45 minutes, until golden brown.

4 Meanwhile, put the sugar, honey, and water in a saucepan and bring to a boil over a low heat, stirring constantly until the sugar has dissolved completely. Simmer for 10 minutes, add the lemon juice, and simmer for a further 5 minutes.

5 Using a spatula, carefully transfer the angel hair nests to a serving dish. Pour the honey syrup on top, sprinkle with the

remaining nuts, and set aside to cool completely before serving. Serve the strained, plain yogurt separately.

COOK'S TIP

Angel hair pasta is also known as capelli d'angelo. *Long and very fine, it is usually sold in small bunches that already resemble nests.*

Raspberry Fusilli

This is the ultimate in self-indulgence—a truly delicious dessert that tastes every bit as good as it looks.

Serves 4

INGREDIENTS

$^1/_2$ cup dried fusilli

4 cups raspberries

2 tbsp superfine sugar

1 tbsp lemon juice

4 tbsp slivered almonds

3 tbsp raspberry liqueur

1 Bring a large pan of lightly salted water to a boil. Add the fusilli and cook until tender, but still firm to the bite. Drain the fusilli thoroughly, return to the pan, and set aside to cool.

2 Using a spoon, firmly press 1$^1/_3$ cups of the raspberries through a strainer set over a large mixing bowl to form a smooth purée.

3 Put the raspberry purée and sugar in a small saucepan and simmer over a low heat, stirring occasionally, for 5 minutes. Stir in the lemon juice and set the sauce aside until required.

4 Add the remaining raspberries to the fusilli in the pan and mix together well. Transfer the raspberry and fusilli mixture to a serving dish.

5 Spread the almonds out on a cookie sheet and toast under the broiler until golden brown. Remove and set aside to cool slightly.

6 Stir the raspberry liqueur into the reserved raspberry sauce and mix together well until very smooth. Pour the raspberry sauce over the fusilli, generously sprinkle the toasted almonds on top and serve.

VARIATION

You could use almost any sweet, really ripe berry for making this dessert. Strawberries and blackberries are especially suitable, combined with the correspondingly flavored liqueur. Alternatively, you could use a different berry mixed with the fusilli, but still pour raspberry sauce on top.

Index

Index compiled by Hilary Bird.